Tell Me More

How to Ask the
Right Questions and
Get the Most Out
of Your Employees

PRAISE FOR

Tell Me More

"I have just finished reading Michael Sherlock's book and I am absolutely buzzing to "tell you more!" I had been a manager in training for a little over a year before I took on my current role as general manager, and Michael's message resonated with me from the start. I must admit I am similar to the book's character Maria in the way that I assumed because people have always liked working with and for me, that I was developing them in a way that was highly engaging. While I may preach the notion of taking the time to answer a question with a question, reading this book helped me recognize that I am not always practicing that method on a daily basis (and if we are only doing something occasionally, does it ever truly change how things are done?). I have never been so engaged by a book that is meant to be motivational and to teach a type of leadership strategy. So insightful!"

Stephanie Bedus
General Manager, LUSH Cosmetics Shop and Spa (Philadelphia)

"So many leadership books are dry and simply deliver their step-by-step bullets to success, coupled with some analysis and a pile of statistics. This book differs in that it is fictionally set in a corporate sales organization with character types we've likely seen before. That familiarity makes it easy to relate to the characters and helps us remember the points being made in each all-too-true situation. I found myself rooting for each as they explored better methods and earned the resulting victories.

The book serves as a good reminder that respectful listening combined with genuine follow-up and follow-through are great ways to involve, encourage and empower people, whether they fall under your reporting line or not.

The importance of positive relationship development and the resulting value when the topics suddenly get real are points well made in *Tell Me More*. I was reminded that honest, direct and genuine dialogue can transform a potentially negative situation into a positive. Leadership qualities like humility, fairness and empathy are displayed by the characters, as is the payback that can be gained from building such a culture and pushing that down from the senior management level.

An aspect of the story that resonated with me involves our desire to solve problems and execute solutions quickly, without giving enough thought to the development of each individual teammate. We all want a shorter task list and that can lead to implementing half-baked remedies. Pushing back the chair to truly understand the problem, then guiding the person facing it to come around to his or her own understanding of the problem builds confidence and achieves buy-in to the solution. While it may still be your solution, they have arrived at it on their own through the 'tell me more' discovery method.

Finally, Michael Sherlock's story deals with the issues of personal confidence and vulnerability that many leaders feel. *Can I do it? Will my people listen? Can I get out from under my own shadow?* The book describes the necessary transition from executing everything directly to empowering people to find and execute their own solutions. As the saying goes, 'many hands make the work seem light.' This book gets right to that point."

Scott Clifford
Equity Analyst, Long-term Investment Strategist;
Former Global Solutions Manager, Microscan

"I love how Michael Sherlock helps us improve our leadership skills by drilling down into issues using the 'Tell me more' technique, which gets all the proverbial cards on the playing table. Using this fresh approach, the leader's facilitation enables their direct reports to figure out how to address various situations. The end result is that the subordinate gains confidence, ownership, and more buy-in with the resolution, which in turn benefits the leader. This technique could be used in any coaching capacity. *Tell Me More* is an easy and enjoyable read, which helps after a full day of work!"

Nanette Steffenhagen
Healthcare Industry Regulatory and Compliance Support Manager

Tell Me More

How to Ask the
Right Questions and
Get the Most Out
of Your Employees

SECOND EDITION

MICHAEL SHERLOCK

Editing by:
Jessica Gardner
Kate Colbert

Cover design and typesetting by:
Courtney Hudson

Second Edition, October 2018

ISBN: 978-1-948238-07-6

Library of Congress Control Number: 2018958232

Created in the United States of America

DEDICATION

Writing this book has been one of the most rewarding experiences of my life — merging my love of the written word with my passion for leadership, sales and the customer experience. Working through the second edition of *Tell Me More*, in advent of my next books, reminded me of how important these concepts are.

This book is dedicated to every person who leads others or hopes to lead others. I have always had a voracious appetite for leadership training, immersing myself in as many books and training programs as possible. When I see others who do the same, I know that they are committed to continuous personal and professional growth.

I am often asked in interviews who my best manager was. I have two.

John was the manager of the jewelry store that was my first paid job at age 16. Having hired me originally as a gift-wrapper for the holiday season at the store, he saw the spark I had to learn. I took home brochures every day on gemstones, Rolex watches, Lladro porcelain and more. When he found that some of the sales people were allowing me to wait on customers, he put me on the sales team right away. While I was away at college, he would call my parents often to see when I would be home for breaks, always giving me the opportunity to work if I wanted.

Glen was my manager in the world of pharmaceuticals. He pushed me to be creative. He allowed me to fail upwards, always seeing a failure as an impetus to try again. He was engaging and competitive and, although I haven't seen him for many years, I am honored that we still stay in touch.

I am a leader in development. So are you. Together we can continue to Listen. Learn. Lead.

TABLE OF CONTENTS

FOREWORD

I've always believed deeply in the power of people in organizations. Many leaders focus — almost completely — on the performance and wellbeing of ecommerce websites or of the machines that produce their products, while overlooking the real fuel behind the success of their organization: its people. The top priority in my Army brigade of nearly 5,000 men and women was *Investing in People*. I and my leaders demonstrated this through our activities — such as sensing sessions, performance counseling, and soldier of concern and resilience programs. In performance counseling sessions, I would ask a subordinate to describe his or her weaknesses. Several would struggle to confess weakness in front of the person who could make or break their career. To comfort them, I'd share my own weaknesses to show transparency. Then I'd return to theirs to help them advance and grow as a leader and a person. Once they opened up, I'd use the methodology Michael Sherlock illustrates in this wonderful book: *"tell me more."*

Simple in a statement, profound in its application, tell me more is the "key to the city" of discovery, growth and potential which lie within the people we work with each day.

I've seen too many leaders stop at the first answer to a question or feedback and miss the good stuff that lies beyond. I've also witnessed people provide feedback or share their frustration without truly processing their feelings and analysis lying deep within their psyche. This happens because, as leaders, our egos stand in the way of the ugly truth, which is so important to solving problems, developing solutions and helping us improve. It happens because we are personally consumed and want to end conversations in our dead sprint toward the next task. It happens because we are so distracted by our mobile devices and the information overload of the modern workplace. These locked doors to discovery require only this simple quest for more to move beyond and get to the stuff that counts.

Organizations do not stand still. They grow, experiencing periods of change. Many people are resistant to this change and stay in their comfort zones, operating routinely and doing what they have always done. Coupled with this (but often overlooked) is the human dimension of the modern workplace. For example, machines will behave with almost complete predictability, doing as they were designed to do. When they malfunction, a handy troubleshooting guide or skilled technician can bring them back to 100%. People, on the other hand, are complex beings in need of discovery. Seeing them as individuals in our places of work and knowing them as little as we do, they may seem simple and small. The truth is each of them are vast oceans of ideas, space for growth and potential beyond our imagination. They require leadership to guide them through change periods, shedding routine practices and tapping into untouched potential. They require constant growth and should be challenged to become better for their own benefit and the benefit of the organization.

Leaders will succeed when they take the time to explore this human space of wonder. They'll discover ideas and feelings they didn't know existed. They'll foster empowerment and inclusion sought by so many in the workplace. They'll develop team solutions to complex problems, creating ownership and motivation to strive for excellence. The key to this human city *is asking for more.*

Want to know more? Michael Sherlock will tell you. Turn the page and enter the lives of the characters she presents in the second edition of this timely and useful book. See yourself in Maria, Mark or Angela in the pages ahead. Feel their angst and bear witness to their discoveries. Follow their stories and watch how they nearly miss opportunities by not asking for more.

I've always learned by hearing the stories of those who went before me, then imagining myself as them. *Tell Me More* is a fantastic example of this. Michael's educational and entertaining approach to the concept of *Tell Me More* forces the reader to ponder their own situation and, more importantly, replicate the leadership practices of the book's characters.

I've always appreciated leaders who desired more from me, who wanted to navigate my own vast ocean and discover what I had not discovered on my own. I was challenged, yet learned and grew, under these leaders in ways I would not have on my own; as a result, my organization and its people achieved Army-leading performance. Consider this book a leader who sets sail on your own vast ocean — challenging and growing you. Or look at it as a suitcase jammed with your inner beliefs, ego and notions, which need scrutiny. Self-reflect on your leadership as you enter the lives of the characters in the pages ahead. Become them, let them become you. Be coached. Let your own light of discovery be lit.

Then take the *tell me more* concept into your own team and witness the magic. Want more? I do. Let's turn the page and let Michael tell us more!

Colonel (Retired) Rob Campbell

Author, *It's Personal, Not Personnel:*
Leadership Lessons for the Battlefield and the Board Room

A LETTER TO MY READER

I have always wanted to write a book. Scratch that. I have always wanted to have a book *published*. I wrote a book when I was in my early 20s. It was fiction. People with magical powers; good vs. evil. It sucked. All 300 pages of it.

A few decades later I finally published my first book. On leadership. And written like fiction. *Tell Me More*. This is the second edition, out just more than two years after initial release. I have learned a lot of what *not* to do in writing, publishing, and promoting a book through this journey.

I am immensely proud of *Tell Me More*. People often ask me if I am Jane or Maria. Honestly, I am a bit of both, and yet neither completely. Many other characters in this book are based on me in various stages of my career, and a few cameos are modeled lightly after a wonderful team I lead once upon a time. Although some people recognize themselves in a character, they also realize that the characters are a reflection of what many leaders struggle with, whether new to management or seasoned management veterans.

Like the characters, the companies in this book are fictional. They have names that make sense within the industries they represent, but the names and the companies are figments of my imagination.

I subscribe to a simple principle of leadership and sales: Listen more than you talk and use what you hear to guide your path. Listen. Learn. Lead.

 Listen more than you talk and use what you hear to guide your path. Listen. Learn. Lead.

If you enjoy this book, you will enjoy the ones that will soon follow. *Sales Mixology* will follow in early 2019 and more books in 2019 and beyond. Characters from *Tell Me More* will be taking you on new adventures in the disciplines of sales and the customer experience.

If you are willing, a review on Amazon will make a difference in the success of this book, and future books. To submit a review, simply visit the book's product page on Amazon.com and click "Write a Customer Review."

Thank you for being a part of this journey!

Chapter 1

THE BUSIER, THE BETTER

Maria entered the doors of the Philadelphia Convention Center at exactly 6:00 a.m. on a blustery November morning. She had rushed, cutting her time close — so close that she had to forgo stopping at her favorite espresso stand on the way to town. She could only hope there would be time to find some bad convention coffee before her duties began.

More than 9,000 attendees would be walking in the door at 7:30 a.m., ready to network, learn, and work on their personal and professional development. Maria was here as one of 200 volunteers who were about to pull off the 12th Annual Mid-Atlantic Women's Leadership Conference.

Maria had been an attendee at the conference for the past couple of years and, this year, she decided to volunteer. It had been a great experience thus far, and the entire team was smiling and filled with excitement. The buzz of happy chatter proved that.

Maria saw her new friend Joy waving to her. To her absolute delight, Maria discovered after making her way through the crowd to her friend, Joy was holding two latte cups.

"Please tell me one of those is for me," Maria asked as Joy handed over a cup. One sniff of the cup filled Maria with a sense of caffeinated pleasure. Before they had a chance to do more than exchange a couple of quick platitudes, the conference chairwoman got things started.

"Ladies and gentlemen, I want to thank you all so much for the time, talent, and energy you have all brought over the past year to make this year's Mid-Atlantic Women's Leadership Conference a complete success! You may think that sounds premature since we are still 90 minutes away from the doors opening, but we have exceeded enrollment by 15 percent over last year and have hit an all-time-high registration record. We have already achieved incredible success, and the rest of the day today will be the icing on the cake.

"Now, you all know what your assignments are, and once I let you loose, please find your team leader for any last-minute changes or updates. But before I do that, let me leave you with some advice. Today is not just about the 9,000 women, and 27 men," she said with a wink and a smile, "who will soon storm our halls here. It is also about all of you.

"You all volunteered for a reason. Today will be busy and, at times, stressful. Remember, however, that you are not just here to serve. You are also here to network and to further your own professional and personal objectives. You are here to learn.

"Live in the moment all day. Listen to the speakers and hear their messages. Meet new people and learn from our exhibitors. Take the time to savor what this day is all about!"

Applause and smiles abounded through the room. And with that, they were off. Maria and Joy met up with their team for one last review of assignments and responsibilities. It seemed like only a blink before 7:30 a.m. arrived, and the doors were open. Maria couldn't help but swell with pride as she watched the flood of people who were literally lined up at the doors early, eager to experience this day.

Maria's Background

Maria had built an enjoyable and successful career and was genuinely proud of what she had accomplished. Although she began her career as a teacher more than two decades before, after just one year of teaching, she found herself looking for something more. She enjoyed teaching, but there was something missing. And of course, the paycheck alone (or lack thereof) was enough incentive to see what else was out there.

Maria landed a job with a nonprofit credit counseling organization. The company was looking for a director of education, and the fit was perfect. She rose through the ranks quickly, eventually becoming responsible for not only education programs but also marketing, public relations, and leadership for approximately 100 volunteers. Because of the number of times she was interviewed by the local media, she also enjoyed a somewhat local celebrity status. The job was fun, and it helped develop the leadership skills she didn't know she had. Looking back, Maria could honestly say that her years there gave her the confidence to do more than she had ever dreamed.

Headhunters found her and, over the next two decades, she enjoyed positions within a couple of different industries. She met, worked with, and learned from many talented leaders and mentors, who helped guide her through various areas of responsibility. She found a passion for health care, and new doors began to open for her.

People liked working with and for Maria. They trusted her and knew she genuinely cared about them. That, however, didn't mean she wasn't tough when she needed to be. She was focused and driven. She considered herself a leader, not a manager, and she enjoyed much success.

People liked working with and for Maria. They trusted her and knew she genuinely cared about them. That, however, didn't mean she wasn't tough when she needed to be.

Slightly more than three years ago, Maria was introduced to Mark Haddon, CEO of a large vision care company. Mark was a soft-spoken Southern gentleman who had successfully built his business over several decades and forged a partnership with 10 other independent owners to form a consolidated company and partner with a national eyeglasses supplier. Thus, EyeSeeYou was born.

In its first 15 years, the company had grown to almost 300 locations in 20 states, and the coalition of the original owners reaped significant financial rewards. The company was humming along nicely, finding its niche in the industry, and enjoying a positive local community presence.

Mark was beginning to look for a successor, and a mutual acquaintance connected him and Maria. After a few months of discussion,

Maria decided to make the move. It was a new industry for her, but her background could easily be applied in this market.

The company structure, made up of many separate and yet aligned segments, was also new for her. A different person in the same footprint of their original business headed each region of the company. Even though 15 years ago they technically gave up their autonomy to gain the benefits of one large company, they still operated as if they were their own businesses.

None of the former owners wanted to assume the CEO role, and yet none were particularly interested in following anyone else either. She soon recognized that Mark let the individual business regions operate pretty much as they wanted to and only occasionally asserted a company mandate. In other words, none of the former owners really had to deal with a "boss" until she came along.

This fragmented leadership method posed operational challenges, and it took time for the group to find a new normal. Maria was extremely proud of how she worked side-by-side with Mark and the regions to streamline processes and procedures, and over time she gained the trust and support of the original ownership team. It didn't hurt that under her leadership, they also hit two revenue record-breaking years in a row and were poised for a third by an even greater margin. After all, increasing revenue can often calm ruffled feathers.

The main problem for Maria was that as the company continued to grow and thrive, and as Mark began to remove himself farther and farther from the day-to-day operations, she began to feel like she had less time each day to get everything done as she carried more on her shoulders. Maria and Mark had a great symbiotic relationship, almost operating as co-parents of the company, each carrying a portion of the burden. But as Mark would be fully divested before Q3 of the next year, they both knew things had to change.

The challenges of this large and still-fragmented company meant that it was time to revamp and restructure. Maria had more than 30 managers reporting to her, and except for the original business owners, most of the leadership team had minimal experience leading people versus managing processes.

Her team was dedicated, and they handled many things well, but their lack of leadership experience was taxing. It seemed that she spent more time solving problems than working on the evolution of the business. It was frustrating and satisfying at the same time. After all, these people needed her.

As the conference participants began to move from the exhibit hall into the ballroom for the opening speakers, Maria had to stop to take two calls and answer three emails on simple issues that seemed to demand her attention. She knew she should turn off her phone, but she worried what other crises would emerge during the next hour and a half. She decided to put it on mute and see how it went. No need to go cold turkey. After all, her job duties today didn't start again until the first breakout session. She could multitask a bit.

Ninety minutes later, the morning session was wrapping up, and Maria realized she recalled virtually nothing from the speakers. She had dealt with four more crises and had one lengthy texting inter-change to talk a salesperson off a ledge, but Maria should have left the ballroom 10 minutes ago to get to the room where she was to be the facilitator for the first breakout session. Frustrated, and more than a little embarrassed, she hurried out the door before the bulk of the crowd.

Chapter 2

TELL ME MORE

Sprinting downstairs, Maria arrived in a rush to see the speaker walking the room to test the mic and find dead spots. She went over right away to introduce herself and apologize.

Maria wasn't excited about this first session. The speaker, Jane Smith, was unknown. She had a book out but had self-published, unlike most of the other speakers for the day. Most of them were *New York Times* best-selling authors and had landed national and international acclaims thus far. The volunteers with more tenure covered those speakers and Maria reminded herself that next year she'd have a better pick.

Maria didn't know what to make of Jane at first glance. She had seen her picture in the author bios, but you can only tell so much by a headshot. Jane seemed pleasant and had a welcoming smile, but what made Maria smile without hesitation were her shoes and hair.

The craziest pair of shoes Maria had ever seen offset a straightforward and elegant navy dress with simple jewelry. An almost cartoon-looking pink bow sat on top of a wild design of navy and pink flowers. The heel itself appeared to be glass or plastic and immediately made her think of Elton John's famous goldfish shoes.

To add to the surprise, Jane had white blond hair with a shock of pink on the bangs that matched the bow on her shoes perfectly. She was a strange mix of professional, punk, and complete fun. Maybe this session would be interesting after all.

"Ms. Smith, thank you for joining us today. I apologize for being late. I got caught up in the ballroom during the opening speakers. My name is Maria Sanchez, and I will be your facilitator today for this first session."

"No problem! Weren't the presentations wonderful? I stayed through the woman from the Olympic gymnastics team and was very impressed by her!" Jane responded with a bright smile. She seemed genuinely interested in Maria's opinion. Maria herself would have been too focused on her upcoming presentation to worry about what her facilitator thought about another speaker, especially as a couple of hundred women filed into the room, but she appreciated the interaction.

"I am ashamed to admit this, but I didn't pay enough attention to the speakers. Quite a few crises came up at work. They can't seem to function when I'm not in the office. I promise not to be distracted during your presentation, however."

"Well, Maria, thank you for your honesty. But I can promise you one thing. I will make you WANT to turn off your phone today. Let's have some fun."

With that, Jane smiled and walked to get her water bottle and to take her seat. Maria took a moment to review her notes about Jane. She did have an impressive resume, but her book title *Tell Me More* sounded a little wan for Maria's taste. As she rose to introduce Jane, Maria hoped that she could keep focused.

After her introduction, Jane rose from her chair and walked to the podium. She was quiet for a moment, looking down at the podium, or maybe her notes. Maria thought Jane might be nervous. After all, Jane's book was just printed. Perhaps the woman didn't have much public speaking experience. The room was about half-full with roughly 300 people present. That could make anyone nervous.

When Jane raised her eyes to look at the crowd, she was anything but nervous. That seemingly awkward moment quieted the whole room. She had garnered all their attention. And Maria could see that she had done it intentionally.

With a now quiet command of the room, she began.

"Who here has one of these?" Jane asked as she raised her phone up high. All heads nodded, and a few people had low and pleasant laughter.

"Who here remembers a time when they didn't have one of these?" This question received a more mixed response.

As Maria looked around the room, she was surprised to see how many younger women were in the audience. She rarely thought about her age or how the workforce around her now held as many people younger than her as did people her age or older. When did that happen? When did she get older?

"How many of you would panic if you lost your phone today?"

The heads nodded more vehemently now, and the laughter became both nervous and ashamed. Maria knew the feeling. She lost her phone a few months back, and it felt like an eternity until she got a replacement.

"How many of you came here today to learn and expand your mind?" Everyone nodded, and now some with some understanding of what Jane might ask next. But she surprised them again with her next question.

"Let me ask you one more question. Are any of you today waiting on news of a birth or the outcome of major surgery?" One arm shot up near the front.

"Looks like we have a winner! What is your name, and which are you waiting on?" Jane asked.

The woman stood up and said, "My name is Sandra, and my daughter-in-law went into labor this morning." Sandra was practically jumping out of her skin and beaming with excitement.

"I fly out tonight, but I decided it was better to still come here today rather than wait at home all day by the phone. They live in Florida, and it's her first child, so I plan to get there before the first diaper is changed!"

Jane laughed and said, "Congratulations! Is this your first grandchild?"

Sandra nodded enthusiastically.

"In that case, Sandra, you are exempt from my challenge. For the rest of you, I challenge you to turn off your phones completely." Jane paused to let this sink in.

"I want you to understand *why* I am making this request. Except for Sandra, none of the rest of us are *knowingly* waiting on life-changing news. And although many of you think that your companies will absolutely *implode* without you being 100 percent accessible for the next 55 minutes, they will not."

Jane directed a knowing smile to Maria, making Maria return the smile touched with guilt. To look like she was complying with powering down, Maria verified that the ringer was off on her phone. Who would know?

"For those of you ancient like me, you remember a time before cell phones. Somehow the world still kept on turning."

This elicited a few smiles and laughter, and Maria saw a few people start to turn off their phones.

"For those of you who say, 'I'll just turn off the ringer,' be honest. Don't you still sneak a peek when you can? Doesn't the buzz or light of a new message *demand* your attention? Isn't it our drug of choice today?"

People nodded sheepishly around the room, and many more began to power down.

"You all made a concerted effort to be here today. You got into cars or on trains, some came by plane, and some local participants even walked. You all made the conscious decision to come here today to learn. Do yourself the best favor you can during this, and every other session today. Completely unplug. I promise you that you will gain more today by doing that than the potential loss of not responding immediately to a crisis at the office that most likely will be solved by the time you turn your phone back on at each break."

Maria looked around, and except for very few people, she could see them powering down.

Oh well, thought Maria, *if nothing else, I promised Jane I would set the example.* She powered down entirely now. It did feel somewhat freeing, but it was also terrifying.

At this point, Jane moved off the podium and down into the crowd.

"Today, although you may not know this yet, you have come here to learn about the fine art of psychological manipulation."

This elicited some nervous laughter from a few people.

"That doesn't mean that we are going to do something wrong. In fact, I'm going to show you that by employing a simple practice of using one phrase, you will make the people who work with and for you stronger — stronger employees and stronger leaders. You will empower them to make better decisions, and they will begin to regard you with a broader sense of respect than you have with them today. It will make your job easier, will make your successes greater, and make your reputation stronger.

"If only I could also make you be able to lose 10 pounds in the process too, then this recipe would be perfect!"

Maria found herself smiling and leaning forward now. Jane just promised to help her move out of crisis management. It sounded too good to be true, but it also sounded wonderful!

Around the room, heads were nodding, and notepads came out.

"I can see that some of you are skeptical, and some of you are eager. That is all good. If you are skeptical, feel free to interrupt me at any time with your questions or 'yeah, buts.' I welcome them. If you are thinking them, likely someone else is as well.

"Now, how many of you manage people at work?" A little more than half of the room raised their arms.

"OK, keep your arms up. How many of you manage people at home?" Lots of laughter, but almost every hand was raised.

"You can see by the fact that everyone in this room has to manage people in their personal or professional life, this topic affects us all. You can use these techniques in both worlds, at the office, with your friends, extended family, and people you interact with on a regular basis. The only individuals I have not found it to be successful is with animals. Believe, me, I've tried for 16 years to manipulate my cat, Bob. The only one who gets manipulated is me!" At this, Jane put up a slide with a gray cat looking bored and slightly annoyed. More laughter as people relaxed.

"Today is about giving you the first basic tool of how to get what you want and need from the people that you interact with while actually making them trust and respect you more. Would you like to know how?"

All heads were nodding. She had the whole room captivated.

This is getting fun now, thought Maria.

"OK, how many of you, when faced with a problem or crisis, want to solve it?"

As heads nodded and a few arms rose, Jane continued.

"How many of you feel like you are a firefighter?"

Smiles and chuckles were enough admissions.

"How many of you pride yourself on your ability to handle crises and put out fires?" Jane paused as more hands rose.

"And how many of you also secretly wish that the people you work with would stop making so many fires so that you could get some work done?"

Everyone was in total agreement with that question.

"OK, then I have the tools for you to use to make that happen."

At that point, Jane put up a slide that said:

As Maria looked at the slide, and then around the room, she saw that she wasn't the only one who was confused.

"The principles that I am going to discuss concern how you actively listen, what you learn from listening, and how you use that information to lead an individual, or team, to a positive solution."

Next Jane put up a slide that said simply:

Jane continued, "When someone comes to you with a crisis or an issue, stop yourself from your initial response to immediately provide an answer or solution. Instead, train yourself to say the phrase 'Tell me more.'"

She gave a dramatic pause before continuing, scanning the room to make sure she had everyone's attention.

"Your job at this point is simply to listen. And you need to listen with *all* of you.

"Don't listen with half your brain. Don't listen while you are checking your email or your phone. If you are face-to-face, give them your full eye-to-eye contact and attention. If you are both on the phone, turn away from your computer, or anything else that distracts you. Give them all your mental concentration.

"If the crisis was launched at you via email or text, *call* them immediately. Some people want to launch crisis bombs at you to make *their* crisis *your* crisis."

Laughter and head nods accompanied this, and Jane looked throughout the room, showing that she understood and had experienced the same thing. Maria could certainly relate.

"You might think that calling right away will send the wrong message, that you will jump to the crisis, but that only happens when you try to *solve* the issue for them. By following the process to say 'Tell me more,' you will force them the next time to think about *how* and *when* they come to you with issues."

People around the room were nodding their heads, and most were making notes as Jane spoke.

This sounds pretty simplistic, Maria thought to herself. *I wonder if this really works.*

"But asking for more information is only part of the process. To get to the heart of the issue, you must follow all the way to the conclusion.

"How many of you have ever packed a suitcase so full that you had to sit on it to zip it?" Jane asked the crowd and many people, Maria included, laughed.

"What do you do when you can't zip it?"

Maria listened to people shout out things like "Re-pack it." "Leave things behind." "Get a second suitcase." Jane nodded with their answers, and continued.

Jane put up a slide showing an unpacked suitcase.

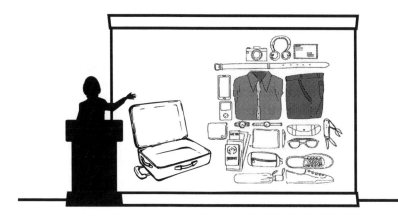

"Yes! You have a decision to make. You have to take everything out and scrutinize it. You have to decide what is important. Maybe everything is, but you have to repack it or add a bag. Maybe some things aren't important and you can leave them behind."

Maria nodded along with the crowd.

"That is the same with helping people to 'unpack' their challenges."

"You see, you don't just say 'Tell me more' one time. You say it over and over, sometimes in a slight variation, until *they* tell *you* that they have reached the end of their story.

"At that point, you still must *not* solve the problem. Your job is to continue the query, but now in the format of a slightly different question.

"Simply ask, 'What do you think (you) (I) (we) (the company) should do?'" Jane paused for dramatic effect, and people were leaning forward.

"If you have done your job correctly, at this point, the person has basically 'unpacked' every issue, argument, and component of the crisis."

"They should see the issue laid out no longer as a box of puzzle pieces, but rather as a puzzle with the frame done and much of the picture starting to come into focus. Most people, given this strategy, will know the right answer."

The next slide showed a jigsaw puzzle with enough of the puzzle pieces completed to recognize a picture of a house.

Jane ran her eyes across the crowd. During the pause, Maria realized her brain just caught up with what Jane had said, and the concept was sinking in throughout the room.

"Questions? Thoughts? Concerns?"

At that moment, Maria realized the tenor of the room had changed. People began almost jumping out of their seats with arms raised. The once smiling and agreeable group seemed to be lit on fire, and she wasn't quite sure how to process all of it.

Why had Jane stopped at that point to ask for questions right now? Stopping seemed to invite an onslaught of resistance.

Jane pointed to one woman who seemed particularly agitated.

"I can see you have a concern! Tell me more."

The woman flew to her feet.

"I have people that I can't trust to make decisions. They have proven themselves inadequate too many times when I have given them the chance to make their own decisions!" The woman's face was becoming red and filled with emotion. Maria had the very same thought, especially about a couple of her less-experienced managers, and she saw many heads nodding in agreement.

During this outburst of emotion, however, Maria was struck by the fact that Jane appeared very relaxed. She was smiling, even though she had gone from a cheerful and agreeable crowd to a mob of dissent. She seemed perfectly calm, but Maria felt anxious for her.

Jane asked the woman's name, and Jillian Matthews confidently added that she was a branch manager at a credit union.

Jane then repeated Jillian's statement so that the rest of the room could hear and then asked the woman, "Did I get all the important points?" Jillian nodded and sat down, arms crossed.

"Thank you, Jillian. Before I respond to your comments, does anyone else have the same concern as Jillian?" Hands shot up around the room.

"Excellent. Jillian, hold tight. I promise I will respond directly to you, but before that, does anyone else have a different thought or reaction to what I've said thus far?" Another hand shot up.

"Let's go with you there in the blue dress. What is your name and what is your concern?"

"My name is Samantha, and I manage a call center for a home security company. Most of the problems my team brings me are simple and should be common sense. If I ask them to 'tell me more,' I'm afraid there won't be much dialogue, or even worse, there will be too much dialogue. I need them on the phones."

"Thank you, Samantha. Does anyone else have concerns like Samantha?" Several hands rose around the room again.

"Samantha, I promise to respond to you as well, but before that, is there anyone else that has another concern?"

Jane nodded now to a woman near the front of the room, inviting her to comment.

"My name is Angela Walters. I'm afraid that if I give my people the power to make decisions all on their own, I won't be needed. After all, my superiors look to me to have the answers and know that I lead my team well."

"Thank you, Angela. Does anyone share Angela's concern?" Almost every hand shot up in the room.

Maria couldn't help but see herself in each concern that had been raised. This sounded like a good idea in theory, but wasn't Jane asking them to hand over decision making to potentially unskilled people without knowing where things might lead?

"Although some of you have other thoughts or concerns, let's start with these. You each have valid worries. And frankly, you have all hit on the key objections I receive when I present the concept of 'tell me more.'"

At this, Jane moved to a slide that read:

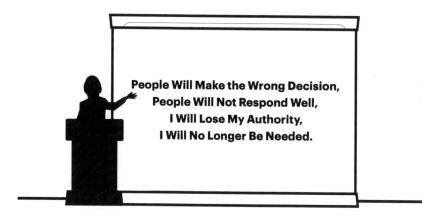

People Will Make the Wrong Decision,
People Will Not Respond Well,
I Will Lose My Authority,
I Will No Longer Be Needed.

"Maria, can you be ready with the roaming mic? I want to get some audience participation here." Maria was embarrassed that she was so involved in the discussion that she forgot her responsibilities again, but jumped up, ready to run. She had a feeling she would be doing a lot of that.

"Let me start with Jillian. You said that you have people that you can't trust to make decisions and that they've proven inadequate in the past when you have given them the authority to make decisions themselves, correct?" Jillian nodded her head, and Maria handed her the mic after a nod from Jane.

"Jillian, tell me more. Please give me a specific example of one person on your team who has disappointed you this way."

"My receptionist is a good example. She wants more responsibility and would eventually like to move to another position within the company. I decided to give her a couple of special projects and gave her free rein to take them to completion. What I ended up with instead was a receptionist who began to wander through the building on 'official business.'" Jillian made air quotes and got a sympathetic murmur from the room.

"She never accomplished either task and was away from the phone and the front desk often, requiring other people to greet customers who walked in or take phone calls that had to be sent down the call tree."

Maria could feel the frustration and anger rolling off Jillian. It was somewhat uncomfortable even though Maria could understand. She had a similar experience with one of her sales reps who aspired to be a manager. Sandra was a great sales rep and could be a good manager one day, but needed time and training first. When left to her own devices, she became bossy more than a leader.

But despite Jillian's obvious frustration, Jane seemed completely relaxed and in control.

"Jillian, tell me more. Did you give her clear expectations?"

"I told her what I needed done and left it up to her to get it done."

"Tell me more. Had she ever completed a project before like what you were asking of her?"

"Well, I don't know." It was interesting how Jillian seemed to deflate a bit at this statement. Some of the wind was pulled out of her sail of emotions. Maria could feel herself relax a little as well.

"I guess I just assumed she did. It wasn't a tough project. I wanted her to speak with our sales managers and customer service reps to identify any local businesses they felt we might be under-serving."

"Tell me more, Jillian."

"OK, I see where you are going here," Maria noted how the fire that lit Jillian before was not burning as hot right now.

"I assumed she would know how to go about it, but I honestly don't even know if she knows how to create a spreadsheet. And since a lot of the feedback from the team said she was acting bossy and often interrupting them even when they were with customers to get information, I guess I didn't make sure she understood good business etiquette and rules of engagement. I've just been so frustrated that she didn't do it right. And frankly, it has made me want to replace her."

"Jillian, what do you think you should do?"

"I think I need to give her another chance but help her to understand. Make sure she knows what to do and how to do it. Goodness, it seems so simple when you put it that way."

"But, Jillian, I didn't put it that way. You did. I just happen to agree with you." Jane took a moment to make eye contact, first with Jillian, and then with others in the room, to make sure they were absorbing what she had just said before she continued.

"The funny thing," Jane started, "is that this method is absolutely simple. It's just not *easy*. What I mean by that is those of us who are *doers* believe we function best when we are *doing*. That also means that when a problem arises, we want to fix it.

 "The funny thing," Jane started, "is that this method is absolutely simple. It's just not *easy*.

"How many of you have ever had this thought: it will take more time and effort for me to teach someone else to do this, inserting whatever *this* is, from making dinner to leading a conference call, than for me to just do it myself?" Everyone nodded their heads, and most smiled sheepishly.

Wow, Maria thought, *I'm in a room with people just like me. I feel like that every day.*

"But if we constantly *do* everything, we will eventually have people who *expect* us to do everything.

"So, let me ask all of you this question. How did I deal with Jillian's concern here?"

"You said 'Tell me more!'" shouted a voice in the crowd.

"Yes." Jane laughed. "I did that. How many times?"

"Too many!" said Jillian with a smile. "No, seriously, you asked me until I came to my own realization. Like you said before, you helped me to 'unpack' the problem."

"Yes. What else did I do, or not do?"

"You were very calm," another voice volunteered.

"Jillian, when I remained calm, and you were more ... "

"Upset. Go ahead and say it. I was working myself up to fight you!"

Jane smiled and nodded. "When I remained calm, and you were upset, how did that make you feel?"

"Honestly, it made me frustrated. I really believed my point was valid, and I wanted to prove it to you. At least that was how I felt the first couple of times you asked me to tell you more. Then suddenly, you deflated my balloon." Jillian smiled sheepishly.

"Thank you, Jillian, for being honest. I wasn't trying to deflate your balloon. You were upset, to begin with, and given the concern you raised, with the emotion you were experiencing, I could have responded in a couple of ways. Let me get your thoughts on various ways I could have responded. OK?"

Jillian nodded her agreement.

"One approach I could have taken could have been to try to convince you first that you were wrong. How well would that have worked for me, Jillian?"

"In the beginning? Not at all! I don't think that ever works. I came to it on my own."

"I could have responded by trying to defend my thesis first. How well would that have worked?"

"I think I would have just shut down and stopped listening to you." Jillian was nodding along as she gave her responses, confident and anticipating.

"I could have also gotten angry. How would that have worked?"

"I was ready to fight. We would have both been angry when we walked away and, frankly, I wouldn't have respected you. Not to mention it would have started my day wrong, and I came here for a positive experience!"

"OK. And I could have given into you and agreed that anyone you have allowed to make decisions on their own that failed you should never be given the opportunity ever again. How would that have gone over with you?"

"I totally see where you are going. Again, I would have felt some small satisfaction for the moment that I was proven right, but I would have been dissatisfied overall that you didn't give me a solution. But by remaining calm and forcing me to continue to unpack the issue, I reached an awareness that I am not proud of. But I am glad I saw it."

"And are you more likely or less likely to act upon a course of action now?"

"I am actually quite anxious to get back and meet with my receptionist. When I hired her, she was the best hire I had in the position in a long time. She did a great job and had a great attitude. The reason I gave her more responsibility was to see if she might make a good customer service rep one day. But now I see that I let my frustrations come through and made us both uncertain and unsatisfied."

"And, Jillian, what will it take for you to go back and start over? How will you handle this?"

"I have a few thoughts, but I want to think it over for a bit."

"I think that is an excellent answer, Jillian because you have a couple of good approaches. But it will bode well for both of you if you think through it first. Let it simmer in your brain for a bit. I bet you'll come to a good solution, but I would also be happy to speak with you after the session today in case you want some other insight."

"I would! Thank you!"

Maria was amazed to realize that this session had turned from a presentation into a dialogue. She couldn't remember being so engaged in a long time. Jillian's story had many elements that rang true for Maria, especially with one of her newer managers. Maria had been trying to get her Utah manager, Elaine, to gain more confidence. She knew Elaine had a lot to offer, especially from her previous work experience, but working in the vision industry seemed daunting to Elaine at times.

Listening to Jillian's story made Maria realize she was just *hoping* that Elaine would find her confidence, and yet Maria hadn't helped her get there. Wishing she had her notebook with her as she ran through the room, Maria started making mental notes on how to work with Elaine starting tomorrow.

Jane took back center stage.

"Now, before we launch into Samantha's concern, is everyone still with me?" Jane inquired of the eager crowd.

Nods and smiles from around the room showed a readiness to continue. One hand rose timidly from a few rows away, and Maria ran with the mic.

"Hi, I'm Sarah. Logically, I see what you are saying, and I get that this is about empowerment. I must admit that this is a little scary. It feels like I'll be giving up control."

"Sarah, great point. Samantha is it all right if we touch on this for a moment before moving on to your concern?" Samantha nodded eagerly. Maria figured they all had the same concern, and it was a logical transition from Jillian's issue, but she appreciated how much respect Jane showed to Samantha by asking her permission to take a side trip.

"OK then. Sarah, tell me more."

"Well," said Sarah, standing and taking the mic from Maria, "this sounds great. It really does." Sarah glanced around the room and saw people nodding along with her.

"But?" Jane asked with a smile.

"But what if Jillian's receptionist doesn't know how to do the task correctly? Or what if Jillian gave you a crazy response to what she was going to do? Not that I think you would." Sarah smiled at Jillian, who gave her a thumbs-up.

"I guess my big fear is that, when I give the answers, at least I can control the outcome. By your way, I can't."

Jane smiled. "Sarah, tell me more. Can you really control the outcome?"

The room made noises of understanding. Maria herself had the same thought, but as Jane posed that question, she had to admit that control is an illusion. It is one that makes you feel better, but it doesn't affect the outcome as much as she'd like to think.

"Okay, okay," Sarah said, laughing. "I see your point. It just makes me feel like I can control more. But my real fear is still there. What if I allow someone to make a mistake because I'm trying *not* to control?"

"Sarah, that is a valid concern. Let's try to look at this from another angle. Jillian, you said you had some thoughts about what to do next with your receptionist. Can we try something?"

Jillian nodded yes.

"Even though you've only had a few minutes to let this simmer in your brain, what is the first thing that comes to mind for you now about how to approach your receptionist when you return to work tomorrow?"

Maria was now running back across the room with the mic. This was fun but getting exhausting.

"Well, I think I need to sit down with her and more fully talk through what I'm looking for in her project. I'd like to have her 'tell me more' about what she thinks is the reason for the project, her thoughts on how to complete it, what she needs from me, and the rest of the team, and help her gain more confidence in what she is doing. Then I need to set regular times to meet with her, so she can update me on her progress, as well as get guidance if she needs it."

"I think you are right on track, Jillian. And what will you do if she has thoughts or plans that you think won't be successful or that there are better ways for her to accomplish her goals?"

"My first reaction before today would have been to correct her and give her the right answer, but I think now I see the value of asking her *why* she would go those routes. It could help me steer her in the right direction. And heck, I might even find she has better ideas that I wouldn't have thought of unless I asked her to explain."

"Jillian, great insight. Sarah, can you see how by using this approach you *will* be giving up *controlling*, but you won't be giving up *control*? In fact, you will gain more control and give more empowerment. That is a recipe for success."

Sarah and Jillian both nodded, and Maria felt herself warming up to this concept even more. It was about a different level of ownership. When you tell someone what to do, or worse yet, *expect* them to know what to do without any guidance, they are not invested in the outcome, or they could be set up for failure instead of success. This simple concept did have some legs to it, but Maria could see how it would take a *lot* of patience.

"Let me explain further," Jane continued. "If I went through the entire exercise with Jillian and then asked her how she was going to handle the situation now that she is more aware of it, there are different possible outcomes.

"If she were less self-aware or a less experienced manager, she might tell me that she was going to give her receptionist another task with more instruction and see how she does. I would not be comfortable with that response because I recognize the likelihood that the result would be the same as it is now."

Goodness, thought Maria, *that is what I was going to do with Elaine in Utah. That can't be my approach. She'll still be as frustrated and insecure as she is now, if not worse!*

Jane continued, "If I don't believe she is on the right track, it is my job to help guide her on the path that has a better chance for success. My role here then would be even more critical than simply listening, agreeing, and letting her go. I have a responsibility *not* to let her make a choice that will be destructive or get in the way of her success if I see that as a possibility.

"In this case, I believe there is one more important step that Jillian *must* take for Jillian's receptionist to have the best chance to achieve success with another project. Granted, this won't ensure success, but it will increase the chances. Does anyone think they know what that is?"

Several hands now shot up around the room. Maria felt like they were in a small conference room around a board table instead of hundreds of people in a large meeting room. People were invested in this message and this exercise. She could see them leaning in as if from around a table.

"Let's pick someone from the back of the room. You there in the red sweater. What is your name and what is your thought?"

"Hello. My name is Jean. I am pretty new to managing people, so I hope I'm not wrong."

"Jean, there isn't a wrong answer. This is a learning moment. Go ahead."

"It seems to me that Jillian could gain a lot of jelly beans by apologizing."

"Jelly beans?"

"Yes, I'm sorry. It is something my husband says. When you do something that is appreciated, it's like a deposit in the bank to be used later when or if you need it.

"My husband loves jelly beans, so he talks about collecting jelly beans when he has done something for someone else. And sometimes he has to spend some of his jelly beans if he's screwed up or when he needs a favor from someone."

Right then, Jean turned to speak directly to Jillian.

"Anyway, Jillian, it sounds like your receptionist is someone you had great hopes of keeping in your company a long time. By starting out apologizing for setting her up with a task without preparing her, and then following up by saying how much you believe in her, you both start fresh. You owe her some jelly beans."

"I think you're right, Jean!" said Jillian. "How often do we as leaders say we are wrong? I think we're too afraid at times. By apologizing, I can also keep her defenses down when I must coach her about some of the things that got in her way of success. That's great insight."

Maria was amazed to see how this presentation had changed and how the participants were actively leading the dialogue. And yet Jane had everything under control.

"Excellent, Jean. That is my recommendation as well."

Jane flipped to a new slide showing a boy staring at a broken window, with a caption that read, "Sometimes you just have to say you're sorry."

"Humans are emotional beings, no matter how much we try to hide it. When we are critiqued, we often view it as criticism. Even the best of intentions with the best of delivery can be received poorly if we don't plan it out. And don't get me wrong. Sometimes we must deliver news that people don't want to hear. In this case, however, starting with self-reflection, and then admitting where we let someone down first, can give us a lot of jelly beans. Jean, if you don't mind, I am going to steal your jelly bean concept!"

Jean smiled and nodded, obviously pleased to have contributed.

"Does everyone feel comfortable with what we have covered thus far?" Heads nodded. "OK, then I want to keep moving on our three initial concerns. Samantha let's move on to you. Let me make sure I can recap your concern. You manage a call center with employees that come to you with simple problems and issues, and that common sense should prevail. You are afraid that if you use this approach with them, it won't be successful, or worse yet, they will feel demeaned by the activity. Is that a correct recap?"

Samantha said, "Yes," just as Maria reached her with the mic.

"OK, Samantha, tell me more."

"Sure. I've already gone through this in my head during the talk and see that my approach will probably make a huge difference. But I'd like to give you a specific scenario and get your thoughts." At a nod from Jane, Samantha continued.

"I have a person in mind who has been with us for more than a year, which is pretty unusual in a call center. She is dependable and puts up acceptable results. She doesn't knock it out of the park but has too many positives for me to want to replace her. My real issue is that she comes to me with questions or problems two to three times every day, and sometimes they are things that we've already discussed. It is very frustrating, and I feel myself cringing every time she gets up from her desk and heads in my direction. To be honest, I am afraid of giving her too much attention with 'tell me more' because what if it leads to her coming to me more often? I hate to put it that way, but it's the truth!"

With a smile and a slight laugh, Jane said, "Samantha, I completely understand. And thank you for your honesty. From the looks on the faces around the room, others have had a similar situation."

Many people were nodding their heads encouragingly toward Samantha.

"Let's unpack this more. Tell me more about one specific issue that she has raised multiple times with you."

"OK. We strive to have another decision maker present during a sales appointment 80 percent of the time. We sell home security packages, and if the husband or wife is not there for the meeting, there is a built-in excuse to delay committing when the person says that they need to talk it over with their spouse. We have constant training for our staff on how to ensure this person will be able to attend the appointment, and a large portion of the bonus structure is attached to this metric.

"Jennifer is usually below average versus her colleagues on this metric and often misses her bonus in this category. She asks me constantly to approve exceptions, asking that an appointment not be counted when she feels she couldn't get that person to attend. I've done it a few times, but it's getting exhausting. Like I said, I want to run away when she comes my way, especially the day before bonuses are calculated for the month."

"Samantha, what do you say when Jennifer comes to you with this? Tell me more."

The whole room, now back to smiling, mouthed or spoke 'Tell me more' as Jane said it, earning the room a joint chuckle.

"I listen to her reasons, ask for justification, and then either approve it or deny depending on if I feel she really did make the attempt. She doesn't always get her way. I think she missed this bonus at least four times in the last six months or so."

"Do you have her sit down when you have these conversations?"

"No. Usually, it only takes a minute or so, and frankly, I'm afraid if I have her sit down, it will just take that much longer and keep her away from the phones."

"Gotcha. I want to come back to that, but right now, here is a hard question for you. If Jennifer comes to you again tomorrow asking you to approve an appointment for her, and you do the same thing you have been doing for the past year, whether you approve the exceptions or not, what will change?"

"Nothing. Yeah, I see that. I'm already living that! But I guess I don't know what to do to change it."

"Why do you think she keeps coming back to you with this one same issue?"

"I don't think she tries hard enough to get that other person to attend. The reps who follow our sales process are very successful in this metric. I am pretty sure she doesn't follow the process."

"Now for a harder question. Whose fault is it that Jennifer doesn't follow the sales process?"

"Ouch. I see what you mean." Samantha turned to Jillian in the audience and said, "I feel your pain, sister." That got smiles and abashed looks from many participants. Inside, Maria was cringing a little too. She was guilty of a few similar transgressions. It is a lot easier to believe the fault lies with the other person, and not with yourself.

"Look, Samantha, I'm not trying to call you on the carpet. I'm just trying to take you a little faster than I took Jillian. The reason that I asked you why you think she keeps coming back to you with the same issue is that it is *your* issue, not hers. What could you do differently tomorrow, based on what you have learned so far today, to lead to a different outcome?"

"Oh ... I see. Instead of asking Jennifer to tell me more about the appointment to approve, I need to ask her to tell me more about why she continues to come to me with the same issue over and over."

"You are right to a point, although maybe not the way you think. But before we dive into that, *why* should you do this? *Why* should you have this discussion with her?"

"I think earlier I might have answered that it was to have *her* admit that she doesn't follow the sales process. That at least would give *me* some sense of satisfaction of being right." Samantha added a wry smile and a little snort of self-deprecation at the end of that statement.

Jane smiled and nodded. Maria was impressed by Samantha's honesty. She was thinking the same thing but felt guilty about that too.

"But I think now I see that although I do want her to recognize that she doesn't follow the process, what we need is to have an honest discussion about *why* she doesn't and why *I* haven't held her accountable to it."

"You're right on track, Samantha. In two minutes or less, give me the highlights for how you ensure this person's attendance."

"You ask, 'Who will be at the appointment with you?' We operate on the assumption that someone will be there. If they answer, 'No one,' or ask why someone has to be there, we explain that there is a lot of information, and it is essential to have the people who will be using the system most to be there together."

"Great. I understand. Let's do a little skill development here for you. You know Jennifer best, so let me play you, and you play her. Ask me to approve an exception for an appointment, even better if you can use a real example, and really play up the challenges you have with her."

"Great. I hate role play!" The room chuckled, and Maria wondered how many times she had heard her team say the same thing.

"OK, here it goes." She seemed to brace herself.

"Samantha, I need to talk to you about the last appointment I just set. The man is a widower, and so there isn't anyone to be at the appointment with him. I need you to approve this exception, so that it won't affect my numbers."

"Hello, Jennifer. Please take a seat. Jennifer, tell me more about your call with this customer. Walk me through the entire conversation you had when you set the appointment."

"What is there to say? I gave you the highlights." Samantha was warming up to her role now. Maria could feel an attitude beginning to roll off her. Maria imagined everyone in the room had dealt with an employee or coworker like that at some point.

"When I asked him if his wife would be at the appointment too, he told me she passed away last year. He doesn't have anyone to be at the appointment, and I wasn't going to offend him by pressing the issue."

"OK, help me to understand. So you asked him if his wife could attend?"

"Yes, just like I told you."

"Jennifer, we have a process for how to ensure that another person will attend. Did you follow that process?"

"Well, pretty much. I mean, he called us after all, so it's not like I had to twist his arm to make the appointment. This one is a sure sale!" Samantha was sitting up straight now, all attitude front and center.

"Jennifer, that isn't my question. Tell me more. When you say you 'pretty much' followed the process, what does that mean?"

"Well, I didn't do it exactly like the script, but like I said, he called us, and he is a widower. Do you think it's right that I offend him by requiring someone to be with him since his wife is dead?" The attitude now became defense with bravado. Maria could see one of her managers, David, in every word and action.

"Jennifer, you've been with the company for more than a year now. I can't tell you how pleased I am that you are so loyal and dedicated to your job. You are always on time; you help your coworkers, are always positive and upbeat. I really value your presence here. But I'd like to help you here a bit as well. Let me ask you a different question. Is your bonus important to you?"

"Of course it is! I am a single mom, and I need that bonus, especially as we get closer to the holidays."

"Is the bonus important to you every month?"

"Yes."

"Do you know how many times you have achieved this bonus in the last six months?"

"Yes, only two. That's why this month's bonus is so important!"

"Jennifer, I would like you to achieve this bonus *every* month. Wouldn't you like that too?"

"Of course I would! That's why I need you to approve this exception for me. I am very close now for the month."

"Do you know how many times a month you come to me to ask me to approve an exception?"

"Well, maybe once or twice. And you know me. It's only when there is no one to come!"

"Here's the thing, Jennifer. I went back and looked at my notes. You have asked me to approve exceptions an average of six to seven times a month," Jane said as an aside. "Samantha, you'll need to find this. I'm making this up as we go." And then she got back into character again.

"Your colleagues ask me an average of one to two times per month. Why do you think that is?"

"I don't know."

"Jennifer, I know this might feel a bit uncomfortable, which is not my intention. What I want to do is help you to recognize what is getting in the way of your success and your ability to earn this bonus every month, on your merit, without the need for exceptions. What do you think could help you to be more consistently successful in this metric?"

"I guess you're saying that if I followed the process, I wouldn't need to come to you as much?"

"Yes, I do believe that to be true. But I think the real issue is whether *you* believe that to be true. Do you believe that following the process strictly would make you more successful? Tell me more."

"Well, in this case, the man is a widower. So, this one wouldn't have counted anyway, process or not."

"Jennifer, does our process require the spouse, or just someone who helps make decisions?"

"Someone to help make decisions. But on the phone with me, he said, 'My wife and I always talked about getting a home security system, and I guess now is a good time.' When I asked if she would be available and he said she had passed away, I felt I did my job."

"But did you follow the process?"

"No. I guess I felt uncomfortable then. I felt weird and didn't want to bring it up again."

"Thank you, Jennifer. That is a great realization! I can understand that and imagine you didn't know what to say. But the reason that you didn't know what to say is that you don't practice the process every day, and so it didn't come naturally. Would you agree?"

"Hmm. I guess so. What would you have said?" Maria had to chuckle at how Samantha threw this back, not as a challenge as much as because she seemed to really be in character.

"I would always go to the process. Like you, if he brought up his wife, I would ask if she was going to be available. If he told me she had passed away, I would say this: 'Mr. Smith, I am so very sorry for your loss. When we have this appointment, it is important that the people who will use the system the most be at the appointment. Are there others that come in and out of your house frequently?' This invites him to tell me if he has adult children nearby or a close friend he talks things over with. If he replied that he was all alone with no one nearby, then I would proceed to schedule the appointment as you did. The bonus is set at 80 percent for a reason. Not everyone will be able to have someone else there. But if you had followed that process, I would have been much more supportive of approving this exception if you were in danger of falling out of range on the bonus. Does that make sense to you, Jennifer?"

Samantha laughed and said, "I'm not sure if Jennifer will get it, but it sure makes sense to me. I have given in too easily, she has given up too easily, and I have not helped her to connect the dots. By the way, that answer was incredible! Can you repeat it so I can write it down?"

Everyone laughed, and Jane said, "If I had a nickel for every time someone asked me to repeat a brilliant performance! ... " Samantha snapped her fingers as a sign of disappointment.

"But seriously," said Jane, "I do agree with your assessment that you have given in too easily, and she has given up too easily. That is a great insight on your part. And back to a question I asked you earlier, why do you think I want her to *physically* sit down for this conversation?"

"I suppose because then I give her my full attention. It is more formal."

"Yes, that is correct in part. But there are a couple of other benefits as well. The first is that by having her sit down when you don't at other times, it makes her aware that this conversation is going to be different. It will make her a little uneasy, meaning she will pay more attention to what she says and how she responds. I'm not trying to make her nervous here, but sometimes a little discomfort goes a long way in establishing a different level of awareness."

"I can see that. I am sure she knows that when she comes to me, I just want to handle the issue and move on. In that way, I've probably let her take advantage of me. By having her sit down, I can show that I want her to take this conversation seriously."

"Yes," said Jane. "And there is more as well." Jane sat right down in an empty chair next to one of the participants and then moved her chair so that she was facing that same woman. People leaped to their feet to watch, even though Jane could still be heard from her mic, and she was being presented on one of the screens in the front of the room. She asked the woman her name and received "Linda" as the reply.

"Linda, if you worked for me and wanted to discuss something with me, how would you prepare for that discussion if you knew you were going to have to sit across from me to present your case?"

Maria had to run to the front of the room and was able to get Linda the mic just in time.

"Well, here, in this room, I feel a bit on the spot," Linda said with a nervous laugh. The room chuckled with her. No one wanted to be in her position even though there was nothing to fear.

Jane smiled. "I know. I am putting you on the spot. How does that make you feel? Tell me more."

"Well, I feel a bit nervous even though there is no reason to. But to answer your first question, if I had asked to speak with you and I knew you were going to have my full and undivided attention, I would want to make sure I was well prepared."

"Excellent, Linda. I agree. Would you be more, or less, likely to bring me a trivial issue if you knew you had to sit across from me?"

Linda laughed. "I wouldn't want to bring anything trivial in front of you. And I like you!"

The room chuckled, and Jane got up, and Linda made an exaggerated sigh of relief, no longer being the center of attention.

"Samantha, when I asked you earlier if you had her sit or stand when she comes to make her pleas to you, *why* do you think I asked you that question?"

Samantha had been standing with a very pensive look on her face. She wasn't surprised by the question, but Maria could see how seriously she was taking this. This was a learning moment for Samantha, and for Maria as well.

Maria couldn't help but wish she was getting this kind of personal attention for some of her leadership issues. The stories told so far could be reflections of many people and circumstances that she faced every day, and now she was craving this one-on-one coaching.

When Samantha continued, she was poised and thoughtful.

"I think you asked the question to help me realize some important tools I have not been using. I must admit now that I've let this happen. I didn't want her to sit down because I hoped that things would get better, that Jennifer would start using the process, and leave me alone. But I've invited her to create the situation that I loathe. I am the only one responsible here. I hate to admit it, but I see it pretty clearly now."

"Now, Samantha, let me ask you one more question. If you handle every discussion like this with Jennifer, like we just acted out, from tomorrow forward, what do you think will change?"

"First of all, I think she'll stop coming to me as often. I not only need to help her accept and then follow the process but also to understand her responsibility. It's really about accountability, isn't it?"

Jane nodded to that question.

"But I think more importantly," Samantha continued, "I won't cringe every time I see her. I see now how I was wished things would magically get better but wishing will never make something a reality. I have a very important part to play, and instead, I've been sitting on the sidelines just watching."

"Yes, you do have a part to play. A very large part, but not the *only* part. It doesn't stop with this first conversation. People fall back into old habits, or they'll tell you one thing and do, or not do, another. You must keep the dialogue alive and full of life. This leads to continued training and development."

People fall back into old habits, or they'll tell you one thing and do, or not do, another. You must keep the dialogue alive and full of life. This leads to continued training and development.

Heads nodded, and Maria saw the wisdom in that.

"You did an excellent job playing Jennifer with me, and I want to point out something else to you. I'm not sure if you realize that you made a statement while pretending to be Jennifer that is very important. It is also likely true about what Jennifer is thinking and feeling. Do you know what I'm referring to?"

"I knew it the moment I said it. She is afraid and uncomfortable."

"Absolutely! People are psychological beings, and we all have our faults and our fears. I imagine the bravado that you played with me is something she has displayed with you before?"

"Oh yes. I've referred to it as attitude, but perhaps it is a defense mechanism."

"I suspect it is. People often have certain responses, that present as an attitude, to hide or disguise their fears. If we want to understand them, we have to be able and willing to look beyond what is initially presented."

The meeting room doors began to open, and people started to filter in for the next session. Maria realized she failed at her duties again! She should have helped wrap-up the session 10 minutes ago but had been so focused that she missed watching the clock. Standing up in a panic, she realized Jane already had things in control.

"Ladies and gentlemen, I must admit that I lost all track of time today, and we have another group coming in for the next session in 15 minutes. I also have to get to my next room."

Maria and those around her were disappointed that the session was over.

"Let me make you all an offer," Jane continued. First, if you would like additional information as well as the opportunity to preview some of my learning modules, then text the words Jane Smith to the number 72000."

At this statement, Jane put up a slide with the information.

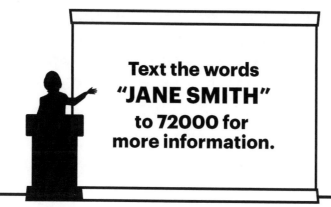

"In addition," Jane went on, "There is a break between 12:30 p.m. and lunch at 1:00 p.m. I will be in room 103 next session talking about change management. If you meet me there at 12:30 p.m., we will tackle Angela's question of how you will look to your superiors. Deal?"

"Wait!" a voice called out from the back of the room. "I'll be there at 12:30 p.m. and think I'll go to your next program too, but you only got as far as point one before we got you sidetracked. Can you at least give us the other bullet points?"

Heads were nodding and voicing agreeing. Jane got a funny smile and asked, "What makes you think there are any other major bullet points? Tell me more ... "

With that, the group good-naturedly got up. The room was buzzing, and people were talking together even though when they entered the room an hour earlier, hardly anyone came in with people they knew.

Maria gathered her belongings and tried to get through to Jane to say good-bye and make sure she knew how to get to her next room. The crowd around her, still peppering her with questions reminded Maria of a celebrity signing autographs. She made eye contact with Jane, mouthed "thank you," and got the A-OK signal, then rushed out to her next room. It looked like she would be running all day.

Chapter 3

WHY ARE WE DOING THIS?

After meeting her next speaker, getting her settled and finishing her introduction, Maria reflected on Jane's presentation and found herself daydreaming. It wasn't until near the end of the session that she realized she still had not turned on her phone, and she barely listened to this speaker.

The session wrapped up a few minutes early, and after making her goodbyes, Maria rushed out to find Jane's next room. Room 103 was close by, but she was afraid to miss anything and found herself running precariously in heels. Luckily, the hallways were still mostly empty.

I wish I could have attended her next session, thought Maria. *I am planning to take my company through a restructure soon, so there can't be much more change than that. I wonder what she has to say on this issue!*

Maria arrived to find standing room only. Jane was finishing her talk, and Maria read the screen.

Jane was saying, "You see, if I am asking someone to change their behavior for any reason, I can't expect them simply to do it just because I said so. Even if they do make the change, do they *embrace* the change, understand it, and *believe* it? Without belief, no change will stick, so I welcome people who question me."

Maria had already seen some of that in action from the earlier session.

"Let me give you an example. A couple of years ago, I was hired to help a large company develop several new growth strategies. We developed a new sales process that people really pushed back on. These are some of the things that people said to me."

As she spoke, the screen showed a slide with each statement.

- I don't need to change my sales process.
  I was successful long before you came along.
- What do you know about this?
  You have never sold this product and
  I have been selling it for more than 15 years.
- This sales process is too aggressive.
  It will cost us sales.
- Why are you unwilling to take my
  20-plus years of experience into account?
  Why do I have to do it your way?

"Sometimes leaders, especially when presenting a change of any kind, are afraid of questions. They aren't confident in their ability to deal with conflict and therefore try to force change."

Maria was listening intently. She didn't want to screw up what she had planned for her own company.

"Examples of how to force change might be to demand compliance, to try to convince those that question that they are wrong, or to defend why they, the leader, are right. They might even get angry, or worse yet, give in and give up on the change initiative if it's not easily understood. But instead, I always say 'Tell me more.' I remain calm and confident, even when emotions are running high."

Maria heard a couple of laughs from the back of the room near her and saw Jillian and several others from the morning session nodding their heads. Their laughter caught Jane's attention, who smiled and waved to the back of the room.

"I see that many from my first session are here and know what I mean. Jillian are you here?"

"Yes! Here I am," Jillian called out with a friendly wave to Jane.

"Excellent. I think what I have been talking about in this session melds nicely with the discussion you and I had earlier."

Jane looked out over her crowd. "We were discussing the concept of 'tell me more' in more depth, and Jillian shared her concerns about using this tactic with an employee who had let her down. Jillian, would it be fair to describe our initial conversation as animated?"

Jillian laughed and gave Jane a thumbs-up sign. Maria and everyone else from the morning session chuckled softly.

Jane continued, "Would you say I was asking you initially to *change* your behavior related to a topic you felt strongly about?"

Jillian yelled out, "Oh yes! Definitely!"

By now the people present from the change management talk were intrigued.

"And would you mind giving a recap of how we used the tactic of remaining calm in the midst of conflict?"

Someone ran up from the front of the room to hand Jillian a mic.

"You mean how *you* remained calm amidst *my* conflict?" Jillian teased.

Jane now gave Jillian a thumbs-up sign.

Jillian, from the back of the room, now had the attention of the entire group, but she didn't seem intimidated in the least. Maria was surprised by how proud she was of Jillian and the other participants from the first session even though she had never met any of them before. It was like they had become a support group.

"Jane, I am so glad I got back here to listen to you talk about the 'tell me more' concept in a completely different manner. We were talking about managing people. Now here you are talking about managing change. And they can all be helped with the same tool."

Jane nodded her agreement.

Jillian continued, "But the key here is to remain calm, and in control I suppose. If you try to *force* change like you were describing, you won't get what you want. If you try to force someone who, for instance, is very strong-willed and believes she is right, not that I know who that might be," Laughter rumbled from the entire room. "You might change action or words in the short term. In other words, you might get initial compliance. But you won't change their minds."

Jane nodded again for Jillian to continue.

"But if instead, you force them to continually give you more information about their thoughts, concerns, or objections, they finally get to what the real issue is. And the only way you are going to get them to unpack their key concerns is by remaining calm. If you react defensively or arrogantly or even give in, you will never get someone to change their behavior."

Jane agreed with Jillian's recap.

"And," said Jillian, "if you don't mind me making one more revelation I just had." Jane gave her the nod.

"By remaining calm and asking the person to give you more of their thoughts, you are showing them great respect. You are saying by your words and actions and tone that you want to hear what they have to say. I might not have noticed that in the middle of the exercise we did this morning because initially I was filled with emotion. And trying to get anyone to step away from their emotional response when they are in the middle of it could be challenging, to say the least!" The room laughed and agreed. "But now I see that you really wanted to know *why* I felt the way I did."

 By remaining calm and asking the person to give you more of their thoughts, you are showing them great respect. You are saying by your words and actions and tone that you want to hear what they have to say.

Maria let this sink in. She thought immediately of Mike, who seemed to fight her continually, even on things that seemed so pointless. Sometimes it seemed like he liked to fight just to fight, and she found herself wanting to say, "Because I said so!" when he continually asked her "Why?" all the time.

How am I showing him any respect that way? thought Maria. *Maybe my own frustrations just lead him to question more? I need to look at this through a different lens.* Her unintended mental pun on her industry made her chuckle.

"Excellent, Jillian. And besides, *you* needed to know *why* you felt the way you did. It allowed you to come to your own conclusions."

Jane paused and looked around the room.

"Folks, we are almost done with this session. Does anyone have any questions or 'yeah, buts' at this point?"

People were smiling and nodding, but no one raised a question. Maria could see people who were from this current session absorbing all they had heard just like she did earlier in the day.

"Then if you'll all allow me a little latitude, I was unable to finish a point with the group in the morning session. The question we left on the table was this: If I have always been the problem solver and I begin to use the 'tell me more' principle to improve how my team makes decisions, will my superiors begin to see me as obsolete?"

Jane gestured to the room and said, "Anyone is free to go if you don't wish to stay for this. I won't be offended."

No one moved in the room.

"OK then! Angela are you here?"

"Here!" came a voice close to Jillian, who immediately handed over the mic.

"Excellent. Angela, you told us this morning that your superiors look to you to have the answers and make the tough decisions, and that you are concerned you might not be needed if you started encouraging your team to make more decisions for themselves. Did I rephrase that correctly?"

"Yep, you got it. But I've been thinking about it since then too."

"OK, we'll get to that, but first, tell me more about the initial concerns you raised."

"I knew you were going to ask that," Angela said with a smile, and the room laughed with her.

"I would say that I pride myself on being the person who has the answers."

"Tell me more."

"I suppose that knowing that people rely on me for the answers and tough decisions makes me feel secure in my position. And maybe it's also a bit of an ego thing."

"And ... tell me more ... "

"Being a problem solver has been something that defines me. My boss often says things like 'Angela, thank goodness you are willing to make the tough decisions.' Just the other day, the president of my company stopped me to tell me how much another department appreciated how I helped them solve a problem. If I suddenly empower everyone else, why am I needed?"

"Thank you, Angela. Does anyone else relate to what Angela is saying?" Heads were nodding throughout the room.

"OK, and before we discuss this, you said you've been thinking about it. Tell—"

And before she could continue, the entire room shouted out, "ME MORE!"

Jane smiled and chuckled a bit, and Maria couldn't help but join in.

"I still have a little of that fear in the back of my head, but as I worked it around in my brain this morning, I see several things. First, if I am the only one who can solve problems, then I carry a lot of monkeys around on my back."

People murmured at the reference. Jane nodded for her to continue.

"Also, if I force people to come to me for decisions, how will they ever grow and develop? I run a sales department with managers that I want to grow and get promoted. But how do I let them shine when I take all the credit?"

"That is a huge realization, Angela, and quite the opposite of your concerns about ego. It is selfless of you and a trait of a good leader. But it doesn't address the nagging fear in the back of your psyche, does it?"

"No, you're right. Which leads me to the biggest aha moment I had about an hour ago. Would I rather be the person who always solves the problem and makes the tough decisions, or would I rather be the person that develops future strong leaders for the company? Both are valuable, but the second can be much more valuable if I can get out of the way of my insecurities. I guess that's really it, isn't it? If I take pride in being the one to always save the day, it is because I am too insecure to trust others along the way."

Would I rather be the person who always solves the problem and makes the tough decisions, or would I rather be the person that develops future strong leaders for the company?

Wow, Maria thought. *I think I better look at myself here too. Am I taking on too much because I* must *or because I am afraid to let go?*

"Angela, I think you are a bit too hard on yourself, and yet the concept is spot-on. Now let me ask you a tough question."

Angela seemed to brace herself, and Maria saw Samantha reach across Jillian to give Angela a comforting pat on her arm.

"Before this realization, if the president of your company wanted you to take some new up-and-coming manager under your wing, how would you feel? Let me give you an example. If he said something like, 'Jimmy in our management training program is showing a lot of promise, and I think he could be something. I'd like him to spend some time learning from you.'"

Jane finished those last lines in a funny, deep voice. "How would you feel? What would you be thinking?"

"Man, you are asking for a lot of honesty today, Jane. I feel like I need to be lying on a couch!" Angela smiled and laughed. "But honestly, before today, I would have probably wondered if my job was now in jeopardy, or if I would be training my replacement." Heads nodded all around the room.

"And how about now?"

"I still might have a little fear in the back of my head, but I can see how putting this into play will not only strengthen and empower my team, it will strengthen and empower me."

"Excellent, Angela. And did you notice that you gave all the answers here, not me?"

"Damn! I see that now! Jane, you really are sneaky!"

While the room chuckled, Jane said, "No, Angela, I strengthened and empowered you."

Although people laughed at this, they also nodded with understanding and belief.

I had no idea that I would get so much out of a day I came to volunteer for, thought Maria. *I have so many thoughts and ideas swimming through my head that I don't even know where to start!*

"Thank you, everyone. I know you are all eager for lunch. In a shameless plug for myself, my book is on sale in the exhibit hall, and my contact information is on the projector here. I always love to hear feedback!"

And with that, the room slowly emptied, participants talking together animatedly with people who had previously been strangers. There was an energy that was contagious, and yet Maria felt a sense of deeper self-reflection than she had experienced in a long time.

As the wave of people filed out of the room, Maria allowed herself to be carried along. She slowly walked through the convention hall, processing all she had heard. Her duties finished for the day; Maria was free to enjoy lunch and the afternoon sessions. She still hadn't turned on her phone and felt strangely compelled to leave it off the entire day. The phone itself began to feel like an intrusion.

Maria was almost to the ballroom for lunch when she heard her name called and stopped to turn around.

Jane had her briefcase slung over her shoulder and hurried a few steps to catch up.

"Maria, you seem deep in thought. Is everything okay?" Maria smiled at Jane's arrival and stopped to allow her to catch up.

"Yes. You have given me much to think about today, and I want to put into practice all that you suggest. My head is swimming with ideas. I'm not sure where to start and how to use this for the things I want to do for my company."

"Tell me more ... " Both women laughed. "No, seriously, Maria. Let's talk. I am in town tomorrow running a management meeting for one of my clients from 1:00 p.m. to 3:00 p.m. Would you like to sit-in? I've been working with this leadership team for several years now. It might help you see what it can mean for a sales organization, and then we can talk over coffee, and you can ask questions."

"I would love that! How much will I owe you for your time?"

"Nothing. If you need my consulting services later, I will make a ridiculously expensive proposal for you," she said with a smile. "Until then, continue the journey you started today. I have your card, and I'll email you the address and details before the end of the day today."

"I look forward to it! Thank you, Jane!"

And with that, Jane was off, and Maria went in just as the lunch keynote speakers were introduced.

Chapter 4

WHAT DO YOU THINK WE SHOULD DO?

The next morning in the office was a blur for Maria. Multiple crises had risen while she was out the day prior, but she was proud of the fact that she kept her phone off until she left the convention center.

She made a few calls on her way home from the conference, handling urgent issues, but the fact that so many calls and emails came in throughout the day made Maria realize just how dependent people were on her. How was she going to take her vacation in March to Brazil to see her stepdaughter? She had promised her husband that she would completely unplug for 10 days.

Although the morning was hectic, Maria forced herself to close her door and turn off her phone before going to meet Jane. She used the time to jot notes, make a task list, and write a list of questions she wanted to discuss with Jane. The last thing she did before she walked out the door was to call Elaine, her manager in Utah, to set a time to do a ride-along. She knew that she needed more quality time with her if she was going to help her boost her confidence and get her region back on budget. Unfortunately, the call seemed to heighten the woman's lack of confidence.

"Am I in trouble?" Elaine asked almost immediately after Maria's announcement that she would be coming to visit.

"No! Of course, you aren't in trouble. Why would you ask that?" asked Maria. And as a last thought, she included "Tell me more."

Elaine paused for a second and then said, "Maria, I know my division is under budget, and we're struggling. I know I am not very experienced in this industry, and you haven't come out to Utah for a long time. I just figure one day you'll need to make a change."

Elaine's comments bothered Maria. Elaine was a good-quality person who was obviously stressed and worried about her job security. Maria knew Elaine needed more support and didn't realize Elaine experienced much angst. Maria took a breath to let it sink in that she had left Elaine out in the cold to fend her herself. It was no wonder the woman felt nervous about a call out of the blue.

"Elaine let's make a deal. If you are ever in trouble in my eyes, I promise to be up-front with you." Practicing a tactic learned from Jillian the day prior, Maria continued, "I must also apologize to you. I should have spent more time with you in the last year. You deserve more of my time and attention, especially since your region is struggling. I want to help you. Will you let me help you without worrying that your job is in jeopardy?"

After another slight pause, Elaine said, "OK, I'll try not to worry about it. I will be glad to have you here. I could really use your help in Provo especially. How long do I get you?"

Maria could already hear a different tone to Elaine's voice and knew she had done the right thing. She agreed to give her a full week, which seemed to make Elaine happy.

"And, Elaine," Maria added, "maybe this will help your concerns a bit. I don't spend time with people who don't deserve my time and attention. I am at your disposal next week, and any other time you need me. Just ask. My fault has been not giving you enough of me before now because you *do* deserve my time and attention. Let's change that and get your team to where you want them to be."

An hour later, Maria walked into the lobby of the headquarters for Home Away, the nation's second largest assisted living and skilled nursing company. Jane was waiting for her at the reception desk.

"Maria, I'm so glad you could make it. I think you are going to enjoy this afternoon. I am already set up, and the group is finishing up with lunch, so let's take a moment so I can give you an overview." Jane led Maria to a couch in the lobby.

"I met the CEO on a plane a few years back, and he told me about the challenges his company was having, particularly on the West Coast. At that time, they were the third largest company in the US and dropping fast. Their competition was opening brand-new facilities throughout the country, and it was getting tough to convince people to send their loved ones into their older facilities.

"Matt's management team was relatively untenured, and each region was operating independently of the whole. The year prior, Matt had to make some cuts to the operating budget, so the frequency of meetings and trainings went down to virtually nothing, which alienated each region from the corporate office as well as from each other.

"I received a call from him a few days after we met, and he asked me to help him develop a plan to turn things around. I'm pleased to say that in a little more than two years, we have reduced turnover at the management level dramatically, the company met and then exceeded revenue budget, and their increased performance and fiscal health allowed them to acquire another small company, securing their place now as the second largest in the industry in the US.

"Once a quarter, I have all of the senior managers come together. Until a year ago, I ran each meeting to help set the stage for how they should run. I worked individually with each person on the executive team to prepare for the meetings. I wanted them armed with the information they needed to participate fully, wanted them ready to present individual department issues in a focused manner, and worked to develop the mindset to help the team operate in growth mode.

"About a year ago, I began to hand off more and more of the agenda to the management team itself. Today my portion is only two hours, and next quarter, I will only come to observe. After that, they will be on their own. My time with them will be done.

"Today I am going to have them share their successes and challenges from the past quarter as well as current issues. Do you have any questions?"

"No," said Maria. "I am just curious to watch."

With that, Jane led Maria to the elevators and then to a large conference room with a great view of downtown Philadelphia. This new building on South Street overlooked the Schuylkill River and the newly expanded biking and running trail, a clear tribute to the growing and thriving community.

Maria assumed she would sit in the back of the room, but Jane directed her to a seat right in the middle of all the action.

"Everyone, this is the woman that I told you would be listening in today. I met Maria yesterday at the conference and thought she could benefit from hearing some of your stories."

Maria received nods and welcoming smiles from around the room.

"Would anyone be willing to tell Maria what you thought the first time you sat around this table a few years ago? You all know I can take it. Be honest." Jane smiled, and the group smiled right back at her.

"All right, I will start off," said the man directly across from Maria. "No one here will be the least bit surprised by my answer."

The group gave a knowing chuckle.

"My name is Jon Pace, and I am responsible for admissions and census in our facilities. My job is to make sure that we get people to choose our facilities instead of our competition and for making sure our facilities are as full as possible. One hundred percent census means that every bed is filled. One hundred percent census in every building, every day, is our objective." Jon said this last statement with obvious pride.

"When we first met Jane, my census was about 62 percent, which is lethal in our business. I had a great deal of turnover with my staff, and virtually no one was following our process for tours and follow-up. I was at my wit's end, and the last thing I wanted to do was to dedicate two days to a meeting at corporate to talk about talking." Jon paused for a moment to give Jane a dazzling smile.

"It's OK, Jon. Your feelings were not very secret at the time."

Everyone laughed a bit harder at the agreement from Jane.

"I am pretty sure I fought Jane the entire first day."

"And most of the second if I recall," replied Jane.

"OK, I owe you that. During lunch on the second day, a call came in from one of my marketing directors, Amy, in the West. She was upset because she wasn't going to make her bonus for the month because, in her words, 'those damn social workers screwed up my admission during intake and the patient's family decided to take her to Care Centers instead.'" Jon had a funny, bitter twist to his face as he mimicked this statement.

"Jane had been making us role-play all morning on 'tell me more,' so before I even knew what I was doing, I just fell into it."

Maria could understand that. She did the same thing when her son had called last night. He was lamenting about his job, his boss, and the injustices of the world. Before she even thought about what she was doing, she said 'tell me more.' It led to one of the best conversations they had had in years. It wasn't easy to move out of the motherly advice role, but the outcome sure was better this way.

Jon continued, "Before that day, my typical reaction would have been to seek a rapid solution to what I saw as an immediate crisis and threat. I would have promised to approve her bonus to keep her calm and happy. I was having a hard time keeping people in that position across the country, and she was doing a great job after just four months or so. I did not want to lose her.

"Next, I would have called the social workers to find out what happened, likely coming across as angry and upset. In other words, I would have turned this one call and one statement into a complete crisis. And," he said somewhat sheepishly while glancing at Jane, "I would have used it as the perfect excuse to get me out of role play for the afternoon session."

Jane crossed her arms and pretended to give him a dirty look. He responded with a smile filled with boyish charm and was back to the story.

"But instead, thanks to our warden Jane over there, I was saying 'tell me more,' which turned out to be the best move I could have made. Amy started to give me more of the story, and I just rolled with it. I had her tell me everything, asking for more details, more clarification until she got everything out."

At this point, Jon seemed to collect his thoughts and took a deep breath. Whatever he was going to say next was clearly something he did not want to admit.

"Then I took a leap-of-faith. I asked Amy what she thought was the best course of action."

Jon impressed Maria. He was a confident and assumingly competent manager. Just by his presence, she could tell that he was passionate about his job and responsibilities. Jon didn't seem opposed to new strategy, but before Jane came along, he, like Maria, probably didn't realize he might be off the mark at times.

"Amy's response at that point had nothing to do with her bonus and everything to do with her thoughts on how to make sure that this issue wouldn't happen again. She even had a couple of ideas to make the handoff from the hospital's discharge staff and our in-house social work department more effective. She blew me away! She had great ideas and asked if she could talk it through with our social workers right then. She was excited and energized when just a few moments before she had been angry and unhappy.

"I gave her the green light and told her to let me know if she needed anything from me. I had to keep her on the line to say I would approve her bonus. She said, 'Oh yeah! That was why I called, wasn't it? Thank you!' and hung up.

"I came back from lunch with my tail between my legs and fessed up to the entire team."

The look Jon gave Jane then was both of criticism for himself and respect for her.

"Thank you, Jon. I'm so pleased you shared that story. How do you use the process now in your day-to-day operations?"

This question seemed to give him back all his confidence, and he sat up a bit straighter as he spoke.

"More than anything, it has made me calmer. I am slightly animated at times."

"No! Not you!" came the response from nearly everyone around the table.

More laughter and smiles proved to Maria the mutual respect in this room. It was fun to observe. She wanted this for her team.

"I knew I shouldn't have started today," Jon said good-naturedly. "But seriously, I have come to realize how I always used to operate in crisis mode, all the time. I always felt I was running as hard as I could, but it was never enough. I began to slow myself down and saw what it did for me and my peace of mind, not to mention my effectiveness when I took time to listen actively.

"But what surprised me most was what it did to the people around me. Since I was always in crisis mode, the others around me always were as well. Sometimes I think it was the only way they could get my attention."

Maria sat up with that statement. She could see herself in what Jon just said, which gave her great pause. Maybe all the dependence on her, the constant crisis mode, was her doing, not theirs.

Jane asked him, "How did your team respond to the change in you?"

Jon paused for a moment, reflective. "That was very interesting. At first, people were uncomfortable with the change. The person they knew always made decisions fast and was ready to move quickly to the next problem. I think people also used that trait in me to get me to react in certain ways at certain times."

Maria understood that. She liked to cross things off her to-do list and sometimes felt people brought her issues when they knew she was bogged down with something bigger and they could get the solution they wanted because she was distracted.

"When I slowed down and asked them to explain in more detail and come up with possible solutions themselves, they didn't know how to react. It wasn't the reaction or response they were used to with me, and it made many of them nervous. A few people asked me if they were in trouble, or if they should be worried about their job."

It's just like Elaine, thought Maria. *I better keep that in mind as I start this path. Learn to anticipate what people are going to think and say when I begin operating differently with them.*

"But after only about a month, my team started to change as well. They came to me with fewer crises and more requests to collaborate. I saw them begin to relax when I came into their facilities when I know that before that, my arrival just meant more stress.

"I am by no means perfect, and neither is my team, but our census is now consistently running at least 86 percent, and we are more aligned as a team to keep going until we hit and stay at 100 percent in every location."

"Fantastic, Jon. I am pleased. Anyone else?" Jane worked the room.

"I'll chime in, although I think Jon hit the highlights that we can all relate to." This woman sat right next to Jon.

"I think we've all experienced the same kind of results. I'm Carol, and I head up HR. When Jane first came, I was thrilled. I love this stuff. Can't get enough of it. But when she first met with us, I believed she was preaching what I already practiced. After all, in HR, we deal with people every day, and I am always trying to ask questions rather than lead, especially if we are discussing a personnel issue."

Carol's admission of feeling like she already did this to some extent was an excellent reminder to Maria that she almost dismissed Jane's concept at first too, relying on the success she already had in her career and in the number of people who respected her and liked working for her.

"One instance made me realize that although I communicate well and carefully with our frontline staff, I was not doing so well with the midlevel managers, and definitely not with my peers here in this room.

"There are a lot of functions to HR, and sometimes HR has to be the final answer. We set policies and really believe we do what needs to be done for the good of our company and employees. Sometimes that gets us in the habit of simply acting. We can't always get consensus on every issue, but we also shouldn't be dictators.

"My big aha moment came about a week after our first meeting with Jane. I had just sent out the updated travel and expense policy to the company. I was proud of it. I had worked on it for months with the CEO and the VP of finance. We had come up with several new ways to control costs that could have a serious impact on our profitability, and I believed they would be well-received by the field with virtually no downside."

Maria could hear the resignation in Carol's voice and knew before she spoke that whatever she was about to share, this was a tough lesson for her.

"I was wrong. One of the changes that I thought was particularly good was a change to the approval process. We felt that if we limited certain approvals, including expense reports, to a few key individuals, it would not only free up more time in the field but would also give us more control over one-off expenses. I sent out the email with the new policy and prepared to move on to the next item on my to-do list.

Three or four minutes later, my phone started ringing. I had angry department managers and regional administrators calling to ask why they were stripped of authority. They were upset and fearful that this signaled a start to change the chain of command and laying people off."

Again, Maria thought of Elaine and how one call to offer her help made Elaine concerned about her job. *People really are fearful, aren't they?* thought Maria. *If so many of our employees are afraid for their jobs, what are we doing as leaders to allow this fear to grow?*

"In those moments, I didn't remember anything about what Jane had told us. I just tried to play firefighter. At the end of the day, I sat in my office with the door closed hoping the phone was finally done ringing when one of my colleagues at this table knocked on the door, came in, and sat down. We just stared at each other for a moment."

"To save Carol a little face here at this moment," Jon said, interrupting, "before this 'tell me more' stuff came along, I would have barged in her door the moment my phone started ringing and demanded to know why she made my life crazy that day. But since I had been fielding my own angry calls that day too, and I was practicing my new skill set, I thought I should keep it going with Carol."

"Thank goodness you did, Jon. I felt beaten and bruised already, and when you darkened my doorway, I was more than a little anxious." She smiled at him, and he acknowledged with a head nod.

Everyone chuckled.

"But all he said was 'tell me more,' and I started to give all the reasons why I had written the policy, why I thought it was good, and why I didn't think anyone would be upset. He very politely did not call me out for my sounds of blah, blah, blah. When he kept repeating 'tell me more,' I finally got it." Carol's smile was genuine.

"When he asked me what I was going to do, I realized that I owed him, and the other people at this table, a big apology. If I would had shared the policy with them first and asked for input, we could have disarmed quite a few of the land mines.

"I wouldn't have needed to change any of the policies, but I could have developed talking points and enlisted the help of this team, and then the midlevel managers, to help their teams understand the changes and not see them as a negative.

"It doesn't matter that my intentions were good. I hate the fact that my lack of communication and discussion led to people feeling insecure about their jobs in a time we needed them to feel more secure than ever." Jane nodded her silent support.

"Thank you, Carol. I think those are both great examples of how you've developed a new skill set the past couple of years. I know that I have been very proud to watch you all achieve some amazing feats!"

Maria could sense the pride Jane had for this team. It reminded her of how she felt yesterday with women like Jillian and Samantha, whom she had never even met before. She wondered what it would be like to have that same level of pride in her team.

"Now, let's move on to the here-and-now. Let's remember our target. One hundred percent census in every building, every day."

"Wait. I am sorry to interrupt," Maria said. She was a bit embarrassed when all eyes turned her way, but she couldn't help but ask something that had been on her mind.

Jane looked at her and nodded, encouraging her to ask her question.

"How can you strive for 100 percent census every day in every building? Isn't that a bit lofty? Aren't you setting yourself up for disappointment?"

Maria wasn't sure of the protocol for interrupting and inserting herself into the meeting, but this group felt so open that she felt empowered to ask.

"I'd like to answer that question if I may," said a man who hadn't spoken yet. "I had the same feelings and questions when Jane showed up. The first time I met her, I thought she was too inexperienced in our industry to know what was possible."

Maria had a sneaking suspicion that this man was the CEO.

"You see, she explained it in a way that changed my view, and the view of everyone in this room. Why shouldn't we strive for 100 percent in every facility every day? The fact that it might not happen has nothing to do with the fact that it is possible. And if we are striving for 100 percent every day, we never get complacent. At these meetings, we come together to continue to think differently and to gain help, ideas, and support from each other. We make sure we all have the same message as we work with our teams. It keeps us united."

That made sense to Maria, and she nodded that she understood.

"However, there is something we do know. One hundred percent census is not possible if we don't provide great care. It isn't possible without a strategic sales presentation. It isn't possible without a clean facility. If we fail a state audit, that could close one of our doors. All elements that are important to us affect our ability to achieve 100 percent census. More than ever, we now work as a team to achieve one common goal that, even if we fall short, our aligned strategy reaps incredible rewards for our patients, our staff, and our company."

"Thank you," said Maria. "I think I need to begin looking at my business in a whole new light after today."

"Excellent!" said Jane, refocusing the group. "Now, who has an issue that is in the way of 100 percent census in every building, every day?"

"I need to discuss pale peas, and mismatched drawer pulls," said the woman directly next to Maria.

"All right," Jane said. "Tell me more."

The woman turned briefly to Maria to introduce herself.

"I am Marge Shunner. I am the VP of Administration. All of the regional VPs report to me and the on-site Administrators report directly to them."

Maria nodded her understanding.

"A few of you already know that in our Spokane, Washington, facility, we barely passed our last state inspection because of two top concerns. The first was that the peas served at the noon meal that day were pale in color, indicating that they had been steamed too long, thus resulting in less nutritional value. Anna and I"—Marge nodded at the woman directly across from her—"have been working on this and have some ideas we'd like to discuss with you all.

"The second issue was a note that the drawer pulls in the rooms did not match in several rooms. The inspection team felt that this wasn't respectful to our residents. Martin and I have discussed this as well." She indicated to the man on her right with a nod.

"I believe that the inspectors were struggling to find something to mark us down on because we have made such significant improvements in overall patient care in this facility. However, these are valid points we cannot overlook on our path to 100 percent census in every facility, every day.

"I want to ask the group these questions. Are we too focused on some areas rather than others? Do I have my administrators watching the right things? Lastly, do you have thoughts on how each department can make a more substantial impact on each facility?"

Maria sat back and watched the dialogue as it unfolded with the group. Jane didn't lead as much as help direct or redirect when needed, and she watched the team productively tackle these issues.

In her own company, Maria often felt like each department operated independently, even sometimes antagonistically, from each other. Her last senior management meeting seemed like a boring slide show of every department's updates with no real commitment, energy, or forward progression at all. Everyone was looking out for themselves.

It hadn't been much a problem since the company was still hitting the budget goals, but Maria wanted to move the company farther, and faster. It seemed like "complacency" was the overall theme in her organization.

As she listened to the group, she realized she did know how to move the company forward. She just needed to take a leap-of-faith, get organized, and then roll her sleeves up. She had to move.

She jotted a few questions to ask Jane after this meeting and then looked up to see that Jane had just written a list of items on the board relating to the conversation that had started with pale peas.

"OK, let's recap what you've all discussed and make sure you all agree. What, if anything, are we missing from this list?"

By this time, Jane had a complete list on the board with specifics for each department to focus. Maria took a few notes because, although this was an entirely different industry from hers, it was still very similar. After all, sales is sales.

"Does anyone have anything to add, change, or delete?" Jane scanned the room. Heads were nodding in agreement to the list.

"Now, this is a great list of action items, but the last line is the most important. What are we going to do to ensure this?" Jane inquired while she pointed to the board.

On the board was this line: "Our Objective is to Increase Results, Not Add to Activity."

This was a great reminder to Maria, who took another minute to read through the list they had just created. Their plan involved tasks and meeting agenda items, and each could easily just become another task just for the sake of the task. How could they ensure that there would be a measurable or quantifiable result?

Several of her managers always seemed to be "busy," but Maria wasn't certain what they were doing to make themselves so busy, especially in the regions where they were under budget. She would have to keep this in mind as she started to take them through a restructure and then a new path for growth.

After the meeting wrapped up, Maria and Jane said their good-byes and headed to a quaint coffee shop across the street. Jane ordered their drinks, while Maria went to snag a couple of comfortable-looking chairs near the fireplace.

As Jane arrived with their coffee, she asked, "What did you think?"

"Thank you so much for letting me sit-in today. I learned a great deal, especially seeing how each person was focused on common goals and solutions. It made me think about my own company and what I want to achieve with it but have been too hesitant to start."

"Tell me more," Jane said with a smile.

Maria went on to share the thoughts that had bubbled through her mind the past two days, especially the fact that everyone in her company seemed very pleased with the status quo.

"It's not like I want to turn everything on its head, but it occurs to me that if we've achieved this much success in the past two years, we are capable of so much more. I have some ideas on how to help us do that, but frankly, I'm a bit nervous about upsetting the apple cart. After all, it took a lot of time for these people to like and trust me."

"Tell me more. What do you want to accomplish?"

"For starters, I need to revamp the reporting structure. I have more than 30 sales managers reporting directly to me, and will soon add the other department managers as well. That is a ridiculous number, yet it was important at the time."

"OK, and then what?"

"I have spent the last two years watching our sales process. It is stale, and we often walk away from a sale because our sales associates are complacent. They make a pretty good living for the industry. They are also extremely dependent on advertising and walk-in traffic. Most of our locations are in malls, and this historically has been a key driver for us. They know someone else will come in, so they aren't too worried when someone walks out without buying or when they get their vision tested with us and then go buy their glasses somewhere else."

Jane smiled with understanding. "Go on," she said. "Tell me more."

"There are also many upgrades to glasses we offer which have an excellent profit margin, but sales in that category are feeble. I want to get my team not only to embrace a new sales process, but to see how much they are leaving on the table every day. I want them to have a greater sense of ownership to results for them, and for the company."

Jane nodded her understanding.

"Yesterday in your second talk you put up a list of things you heard from people when you introduced a new sales process. I could hear my own people saying the same things. How did you get those salespeople past those thoughts and feelings? How did you get them to embrace something new?"

Jane laughed. "Maria, you just witnessed part of the answer today. Those statements came from Home Away marketing directors and admissions staff. How do you think we got past it?"

"Oh," Maria said. "I should have put that together. I see now. You taught the leadership team the strategies and then helped them put the other actions into motion. And then you helped develop that leadership team into a group that helped each other as well as the company. I just saw them put their department issues aside for the good of the entire company."

"That's right. But what you saw today still wouldn't be successful unless they created the same dynamic down the line to the people within their teams. They must make sure the same type of cooperation and teamwork they practice now in the executive meet-ings happens at every level of the company.

"If you were to walk into any of their buildings today and had seen them two years ago, you wouldn't even know you were in the same place. And some of the best ideas have come from people in positions who previously felt they had no voice."

Jane could see that Maria was a little confused by that comment.

"Let me give you an example. There is a facility in Idaho. You heard us discuss how the West region was under the most stress in the past few years. These are the oldest buildings in the company, and the largest competitor opened many brand-new built-from-scratch facilities in their backyards.

"When I first met Matt and his team, they were seriously consid-ering closing four of the oldest locations because it was becoming so hard to compete. When Jon Pace finally gave into the 'tell me more' approach, he spent a great deal of time in these four locations, talking and brainstorming with the marketing and admissions people, trying to find solutions for lagging census and admissions.

"As Jon was walking out one of the facilities one day, the recep-tionist, Lisa, asked if she could share an idea with him. Jon, of course, stopped in his tracks and said ... "

"Tell me more!" Both Jane and Maria made the statement at the same time.

"I know," Jane said. "It is both annoying and fun, isn't it?"

Maria agreed.

"Lisa said that the night before, she decided to stop by the new Care Centers that had recently opened just a few miles from her building. She introduced herself to the marketing director and was very up-front with her about who she was and where she worked. She told the lady that she wanted to see what a brand-new facility looked like."

Maria was impressed with Lisa's initiative.

"The marketing director eagerly gave her a tour, proudly showing off the hair salon, the ice cream parlor, the karaoke stage, and more. Lisa told Jon about the tour and how beautiful the building was. He confided in me later that he was forcing himself to smile through the whole story because he was afraid she was going to tell him that she was going to quit and go work there. And if you met Lisa, you would be afraid to lose her too. She is an absolute gem!"

Maria could understand that. She had a couple of customer service people in her stores whom she would never want to lose.

"Anyway, Lisa told Jon that the first thing she noticed when she walked through the door of the other center was the smell of popcorn. It was movie time at the facility, and the residents were happily munching on popcorn and watching a movie. She said she never thought about what it smelled like when in their building, and paid very close attention when she got to work that day. She told him their building smelled like cleaning detergent and sick people."

"Ouch," said Maria.

"Right," said Jane. "That wasn't really what Jon wanted to hear, but he kept on asking her to tell him more, practically pinching himself to keep from either jumping in or trying to make excuses."

Maria felt for Jon. Given what he had shared about himself that day, she knew that would have been very tough for him. She was also fiercely protective of her stores and her people and likely would have felt the same way.

"Then Lisa said, 'I wonder if we could bake cookies or something so that when people came in for a tour, it would smell like cookies. I think the family members coming to visit their loved ones would like a hot cookie probably also."

Maria was impressed and a little stunned. Her mouth dropped open as the simplistic solution to a critical issue presented itself.

"That is precisely the reaction that Jon had, and the same reaction I had when he told me. He, of course, went right out and bought a toaster oven and some frozen cookie dough. They experimented with it for two weeks, and admissions increased. Best of all, the family members that walked through the door felt even better about where they had their loved one, enjoyed the cookies, and spent more time visiting with Lisa than ever before.

"The only downside was that the staff also wanted the cookies, so after a large cookie dough bill, they had another decision to make!"

Both Jane and Maria laughed. That was easy to believe.

"Ask me another time how they solved the problem of the cookie bill. It is another great story. But the end of this one is that there is a cookie oven in every Home Away facility now. It's just one step in their success, but it is an important one. When Jon complimented Lisa later about her brilliant idea, she said that she had finally felt like he really wanted to get people's input. She felt valuable."

Maria nodded. People wanted and needed to feel a part of something.

Jane continued, "And after that, Jon made sure he kept his eyes open. Now he interacts with everyone, not just his admissions and marketing people. He told me he feels like he operated with blinders on, and now he sees that those blinders kept him from seeing the entire picture."

Maria could see some blinders she had on too.

"Jane, you've given me so much in the last two days. I can't begin to thank you. Seriously. I'm wondering if I should ask you for that ridiculously expensive bid to help me," Maria said, only half-joking.

"I believe you are more capable than you think. You can do it. I am here if you need me though."

With that, the women said good-bye. Maria headed home, and Jane left for the airport.

After dealing with a few Friday-afternoon crises and practicing more of the "tell me more" strategy, Maria finally shut down her phone and used her remaining drive time home to contemplate all she had learned the last few days. Her mind was racing, and although she didn't notice, she had a giant smile on her face. She was ready now.

Monday she was going to act.

Chapter 5

EYESEEYOU

Maria left for work early Monday morning. Her husband was almost glad to hurry her out of the house as, according to him, he needed a break from hearing about how wonderful Jane was.

He said this with a smile. Secretly, he was pleased to see his wife this animated. Lately, it seemed like she was tired and stressed. She didn't appear to be having as much fun in her job as she did when she took it, although he knew how passionate she had become about the company and industry.

As Maria settled into her office, coffee at the ready, she reviewed what she wanted to accomplish. It wasn't just about selling more glasses and contacts. She wanted a company that operated like what she just saw at Home Away. After thinking about it over the weekend, she decided that she had three key objectives:

1. Create a sense of team through the entire company, starting with building a bridge between field and corporate staff.
   - Change the organizational structure to support the team.

2. Develop true leadership within the company.
    –   Although we have managers, both in the field and in the corporate office who have managed details and processes to some degree of success, they don't have a consistent presentation of leadership.

3. Empower our leaders, and then make sure they empower our people.
    –   Just as with Home Away, we need people at every level of the organization to feel like they could, and should, contribute.

Once she was satisfied with her objectives, Maria started by calling Mark. As usual for a Monday, he was heading to the golf course. Now that he was semi-retired, he spent two weeks of every month at his home in Phoenix.

"Mark, I'm glad I caught you before you teed off."

"Good morning, Maria. I see the weather hasn't been too bad in Philly yet. I can guarantee it is better here though!"

Maria and Mark had a great relationship. Maria found Mark to be a mixture of a mentor, colleague, and friend.

"Sure, rub it in. But who doesn't love winter in Philly?" she laughed.

"Mark, I know we've talked a few times now about restructuring the company and the reporting structure. I am ready to do it now but wanted to talk it through."

"OK, Maria. Tell me your thoughts." Maria couldn't help but notice the similarity to the "tell me more" principle.

"Well, beyond the actual restructuring, I need to get this group to do a couple of things. I need the entire management team to understand that although we've hit revenue target the past two years, we are still not growing. I want to get them excited about our true potential. We are leaving a lot of revenue on the table in every location, mostly because we are happy with the status quo. Every region is just existing, happy to be on budget. No one is hungry for more."

"OK, what else?" Mark urged.

"I also see a big gap between our field managers and our support services. As you and I have been managing these groups separately, I think we have inadvertently done them all a disservice."

"What do you mean, Maria?"

"Well, I think we have allowed them to operate as if they are two separate teams instead of one team trying to achieve a common goal."

"Hmm, interesting. So, some of the infighting and backbiting is because we aren't aligned?"

"Yes, Mark, I think that is it. I think they feel like they are either on my team or yours, and that puts them at odds. I want to change that, and it means that we not only need to operate as one, but we need to deal with this conflict head-on."

"I agree, Maria. I think you are right, and now is the right time to act. If I am going to retire next year, we better get moving on the transition to you as CEO. How do you want to proceed?"

Although Maria anticipated this response, it was nonetheless wonderful to hear.

"Thank you, Mark. I've got a preliminary plan, but I want to get some input from the team as well. I want them invested in the outcome. I'm going to have a conference call tomorrow to have an initial discussion with the sales managers and then have everyone fly in for a two-day meeting. I would then like to have you and me meet with the support services managers after that to discuss how these changes affect them."

"Maria, you tell me when and where, and I'll be there. But I am going to be quiet. I will be there to show my support, but this plan is yours. I will add my input to you individually, but it is important for everyone in the company see you assuming the role with my support." Maria was quiet for a moment.

"Wow. This is getting real, isn't it?"

"Yes, it is. And it will be fine. Just send me a meeting invite, and I'll be there. But for now, I must continue my tough day on the golf course. Call me if you need anything!"

And with that, Maria was committed. There was no backing down now.

The next day, she had a full conference call going with many happy voices chiming in to say hello to their colleagues. In other words, it was chaos.

"OK, everyone. Thank you all for joining. Instead of doing a roll call, please send me a text or an email to let me know you are on the line and so I can follow up with anyone who couldn't make it for this last-minute call."

Maria's phone started buzzing immediately as it always did at the start of the call.

"I wanted to get you all together to discuss some changes that we are ready to make as a company."

The silence that followed that statement left little doubt to Maria just how much people fear change. She was determined, however, to get her team to work together as the Home Away team did.

"Right now, there are more than 30 of you reporting directly to me from the field, while Mark still manages the other support services managers. As you all know, Mark has decided that his future is on the golf course in Arizona after June of next year. That means that I will have even more on my plate, and I know we are ready to take some giant steps forward with the company." Quiet chuckles supported the teams' love for their founding CEO.

The silence now seemed even deeper. Maria was getting a little nervous but refused to let it get to her.

"We have had many accomplishments these past two years, and I know we are ready for even more. With that in mind, we need to talk about restructuring the sales management team, adding another layer of leaders."

Now the silence was oppressive. Maria could almost hear a few of the folks salivating, eager for a chance at promotion.

"I have a preliminary plan, but I'd like to have all your input. I am scheduling a meeting here in Philly in December. It is short notice, but I checked all your calendars, and no one has requested time off on the 15th and 16th. If you have a conflict I don't know about, please pop me an email, after this call."

Maria didn't let the weighted silence slow her down.

"Between now and the meeting, I would like you all to give some thought to a few questions. I'll send them out again via email after this call, so you don't need to write these down.

"1. If you were going to revamp our sales management structure, what would it look like, and why?

"2. What do you think is the best role for you to play in this new structure, and why?

"3. What do you need from the support services managers to be successful in your current job? This includes operations, marketing, the call center, HR, billing, accounting, and anyone else that supports what we do in the field.

"4. What could you personally do better to help the support services managers be more successful in their jobs?

"Any questions?"

There was a tense silence now. A sense of waiting. Then one lone voice spoke up.

"Maria, this is Kelly. Should we be worried about our jobs?"

Maria took a deep breath. Here was her first test.

"Kelly, why do you ask that question? Tell me more about why you are concerned."

"Well, as you know, I came from another industry before taking this position. When we restructured the sales force, I ended up out of a job. I just want to know if I need to prepare."

Maria could feel the tension as everyone waited for her response. Stealing a page from Jane, Maria asked, "Does anyone else share the same concern as Kelly?"

A few noncommittal mumbles told her they did.

"Kelly, I am sorry that you have that concern. No one is going to lose their jobs. I intend to add to our ranks. But I understand that, given your history, why it would make you nervous.

"That is why I am asking all of you to help shape and develop our future. We have all accomplished a great deal together. I owe it to you all to give you some sense of being a part of where we go from here. When we come together next month, I want it to be an adventure we begin together.

"Does that help, Kelly? Does that make sense and alleviate any of your concerns?" Maria held her breath, waiting for the response.

"Yes, actually it does. I hated to ask the question, but I appreciate what you are trying to do. I'll try to be less paranoid and more positive."

"Kelly, that is all I can ask of any of you. Someone else. What other questions do you have?"

"Maria, this is David. Does that mean I will finally get my promotion?"

Everyone laughed, and the mood lightened significantly. Everyone knew David loved to take center stage. He was always making a plug to be the VP of everything.

"David, you never know," Maria laughed.

"Maria, don't encourage him!" came a voice she assumed to be Mike. "That's *all* we need!"

Maria felt more confident as people seemed to relax a bit. "Anyone else?"

Silence followed.

"OK then, I promised not to keep you very long. I want to have your responses in writing by the 11th so that I have time to read and consider your answers and input. Think creatively and think about what you would do if all the decisions fell on you. Together we will find some unique solutions."

"Thank you, everyone. Call me if you need me. I'll be available by phone for the rest of the day."

And with that, Maria could hear people saying good-bye, the chime of people popping off the line. People seemed to be more positive from the sounds of their voices.

All in all, she felt like she had made a great start.

At that moment, she got a text from Mark with the thumbs-up emoji. She had forgotten he was even on.

Over the next few weeks, Maria could feel a new energy within herself. Her team seemed excited too, especially when she read some of the responses that flooded in within hours of her conference call. It seemed that everyone was excited about putting new life into the company, even if some of them, like David, had somewhat unrealistic ideas of what it would mean.

Chapter 6

THE FOUNDATION IS POURED

As the team came into the meeting room on December 15th, Maria smiled at the buzz of happy chatter.

The day was beautiful, and their meeting room on the top floor of the hotel gave the perfect view of Philadelphia as it gathered a light dusting of snow. There was fresh energy to the city, and Maria took a moment to enjoy the view and a few sips of coffee while people came in and settled in for the day. She wished that Mark was there, but she was confident in the strategy for the day. She couldn't help but reflect on the call this morning with him.

"Maria, if I am there in the morning, people will be looking to me to see my reactions. They'll pull me aside at breaks and lunch to get my input. I don't think we should allow them that distraction. If you need me, call me. But you won't. Let them see that I trust you enough not to look over your shoulder."

Maria had to admit that Mark was right, but she missed his presence. Although she knew she had his full support, she hadn't realized just how much she valued his belief in her.

"Besides, you have a good plan here," Mark had added. "I will do my part with the department managers. You'll be great."

After thinking more through her strategy and goals, the activity she would do with the sales managers this morning would parallel what Mark would do a few miles away. If they were both successful, they'd have an excellent foundation for the company to work together, not against itself.

"Should I be ready with my acceptance speech?" David's voice brought Maria out of her reflection, and she turned to greet him. David was a presence all in of himself. He entered a room like he was a king and loved to be the center of attention. He could make you nuts at times, but Maria couldn't help but like him. He made you smile, ... when you didn't want to wring his neck.

"Good morning, David. What do you think you'll need a speech for?"

"For when you promote me to vice president of the company, of course! Are you planning to make that announcement today or wait until tomorrow?" David said this all with a grin that would have suited a presidential candidate. All he needed was a hand to shake and a baby to kiss.

"David, I think you better leave any speeches in your coat pocket today. That isn't on the agenda." She told him this with a smile and walked to the front of the room.

"Everyone, I want to get started in two minutes please, so grab any last-minute coffee refills or another pastry."

It didn't take long for everyone to take their seats, and soon they were ready to go.

"First of all, thank you for coming on short notice. We have a lot to cover the next two days, and I want to have some fun as well."

Maria saw a few cell phones out on the tables, making her sure her next move was right on point.

"Here is our first activity. I need everyone to pick up their phones." People looked confused but did as she asked.

"I want everyone to power down and place your phone in this basket." Maria handed the basket to David, who was, of course, sitting closest to her.

People looked genuinely confused and a little panicked.

"What?" "Really?" came the responses from around the room.

"What if there is an emergency?" asked another.

"Folks, believe it or not, our entire company will not fall apart before 10:00 a.m. I will let you have your phones during each break, but not while we eat lunch. Today we are going to focus on the business, and on each other as a team. I want your full and undivided attention. I want you all to be completely present."

Maria almost laughed as she saw how people put their phones in the basket, nearly caressing them as if they were saying goodbye to a loved one. She couldn't fault them. She had felt the same way only a few weeks ago.

Once the phones were collected, Maria went in for the kill.

"And now, all laptops and tablets go into briefcases. Today is a technology-free zone. No email, no typing, no beeps, no buzzing, no nothing."

This caused an even greater reaction, and now Maria did laugh out loud.

"Come on now, people! I haven't asked you to cut off your right arms. It just feels that way. Today we are doing something different, and you'll thank me for it. Eventually."

Roger, one of the original founding members of the company, gave her a thumbs-up sign and had a giant smile on his face. He was eating this up. She could always count on Roger to not only be in her corner but also be the first to try anything that would help his team. He was a true leader.

Once the tables held only coffee, pastries, and notepads, Maria began. There was no turning back now.

Maria grabbed the bag of jelly beans she had been hiding in her brief-case. She took one of the water glasses from a table, filled it with as many jelly beans as it would hold, and set it on the projector cart.

Everyone was puzzled, but she gave no explanation and started the meeting.

"Today we begin to take our company to new heights. The past two years have proven to us all that we can hit basic sales expectations. We are on track to hit our budget goals for the third year in a row, and our sales force is producing at a steady pace.

"The thing is; we aren't growing. Our budget has had zero growth objectives for the last two years. In other words, we are hitting numbers that we should have hit three years ago. That means the company is stagnant, our sales force is stagnant, and all incomes related to the company and our people, including ours, are stagnant."

Maria paused for a moment to let her words sink in. She could see how bold statements followed by a dramatic pause made people pay attention. She had wondered about starting so directly, but she figured if she was going to mix things up, then she had to do it from the outset. Besides, she had already shocked them by removing their lifelines to the outer world.

"How do you all feel about what I've just said? I'd like to know your thoughts."

"I want to know about the jelly beans," said David. Maria smiled and turned his way.

"You'll understand about the jelly beans later, David. Right now, I want to know what people think and feel about what I just said about our company."

Maria left the question out there. The room was quiet for what seemed like an eternity. The group that was noisily chatting as they entered the room this morning was quite suddenly shy.

"Come on, people. I want to know your thoughts," said Maria, deciding to sit on the edge of the table at the front of the U-shape design. Perhaps if she sat down, it would seem less like a classroom.

"I'll begin," said Roger. Maria gave him both a nod and an private prayer of thanks.

"My little portion of the world in our company has always done pretty well. I have a great team with a lot of tenure. We enjoy a nice reception in our community. And I've been thrilled that the company has hit budget the last two years." Roger smiled but seemed thoughtful.

"But I think you are right," Roger continued. "My folks are great, but I sense malaise in them. It's not that there is anything wrong, but we don't have a fire anymore."

"Thank you, Roger. Tell me more."

"Well, I know they are happy. They make a nice living. And they are fabulously dependable. But 10 to 12 years ago, we were having lots of fun! Now it seems like another day at the office."

"Great, Roger. I know that not everyone has a team as tenured as yours. Can you help us out a little further? Tell me more about what it was about 10 to 12 years ago that was different from today."

"Back then, the company was just starting. EyeSeeYou was in its infancy. We were making the change from being a local business I owned to become a part of something bigger. Some things were better; others were not; overall it was exciting."

"Excellent, Roger. And what do you think would give that fire back to your team?"

"I loved the questions you had us answer before this meeting. It is always a bit daunting to think of change, especially change with the organizational structure, but at the same time, it would be new. Exciting. We'd have something to break the monotony. And if we are also doing that to increase sales and revenue, that means more money for everyone. That should get some people interested at least."

"Thank you, Roger. Who else? What are your thoughts when I talked about us being stagnant as a company?"

Mike spoke from the far end of the table. "Well, I don't want this to sound bad or anything, but I guess my first reaction is, why do we have to do anything different? Things are going well, and I am busier than ever. I have a lot of stores, some doing well, others not so well. I've got a lot on my plate right now. If we start shaking things up, where will that lead us?"

Maria knew there would be resistance and thought she was ready for it, but she couldn't help the pang of disappointment to get this response so soon. She took a deep breath and practiced being calm.

"Mike, thank you for your thoughts. Tell me more. What concerns you about change?"

Mike seemed to be ready for her question and got a little fired up.

"Well, for one, I am finally fully staffed. We've had a lot of turnover in Minnesota the last few years. I've worked hard to get a full crew that looks like they'll stay awhile. If we start introducing new things, they could get scared and leave."

"Mike, tell me more. Why do you think people would leave if we start introducing new things?"

"Well, I'm not sure what you are planning to do here, so how could I even know? I just know that people don't like change, and I don't want us to become some crazy sales machine that no longer cares about its customers!"

She could see that Mike was getting worked up to fight her. He often did, but others seemed to be nodding along with him as well.

Maria was having fun now even though she was still a little nervous. She was beginning to appreciate just how much control you have when emotions drive people around you. It was time to see just how much she had learned from Jane. She took her time before she spoke.

"Mike, what have I said that would make you think we are going to do anything that would make us no longer care about our customers? Tell me more about what you are thinking." The calm in her voice made her proud. A month ago, she would have reacted on the spot.

Out of the corner of her eye, Maria saw Roger write something down. He looked up and gave her a wink. He was already beginning to see what she was doing. She wondered how long it would take the others.

"Well, you are talking about growth, and we all know that means more money. You'll expect us to sell more. And to sell more, we are going to have to become pushy salespeople. I didn't sign up for that!"

Now as Maria looked around the room, some of the people who had been nodding along with Mike had different looks on their faces. Elaine, for one, seemed poised to say something, her head cocked to the side.

"Elaine," asked Maria. "Do you have a thought? You seem to have something you want to add."

Elaine gave her a somewhat uncertain look but went ahead.

"Mike, Maria didn't say anything about becoming pushy salespeople. She is talking about growth. In the medical spa industry that I came from, we introduced new products and processes all the time, trying to both stay current as well as continue to grow. We were able to do it without becoming pushy. We spent a great deal of time in our leadership meetings working together to craft solutions as well as head-off any problems. I don't see why we couldn't do the same thing here."

Maria made a mental note to compliment Elaine during the break for her insight. Her willingness to challenge a colleague showed she was already gaining confidence.

Mike didn't seem convinced, however. Maria went another step.

"Mike, if you think change and a desire for growth will make us pushy salespeople, what do you suggest that we do?"

That question threw him. He wasn't ready for solutions. He only wanted to fight.

"Well, I don't know, but I don't know that we need to upset the status quo."

Maria decided to open it to the group further.

"Does anyone else have any thoughts on the matter?"

"I do," said Jesse. Jesse was a strong manager and leader and had been with the company for more than 10 years. His peers and his team respected him. He also had a charming Southern drawl, making it easy to listen to him and difficult to disagree.

"I have some great salespeople too, Mike, and I hear what you are saying. Change can be daunting. But I believe my team can handle a new challenge. I have the top three producers in the company in my region. If I offer them ways to be even more successful, they will jump at it. And then others will be interested. I think we can make growth an exciting initiative." Maria could always count on Jesse. He might be quiet at times, but when he spoke, it carried weight.

"Besides," he added, "I would like to buy a new pontoon boat next summer. Can we start making more money soon enough to do that?"

The group laughed with him, and Maria nodded enthusiastically.

"I think we can certainly give it a try, Jesse! Who's in?"

And with that, almost everyone seemed interested. Even Mike perked up at the mention of more money. Less than 30 minutes into the day, Maria was hopeful they could achieve all she wanted for this meeting, but she knew she had a few more challenging surprises for them. She wondered how they were going to handle all that she planned to throw at them.

Maria put the questions she had asked earlier on the screen and gave everyone a minute to review.

- If you were going to revamp our sales management structure, what would it look like, and why?
- What do you think is the best role for you to play in this new structure, and why?
- What do you need from the support services managers to be successful in your current job? This includes operations, marketing, the call center, HR, billing, accounting, and anyone else that supports what we do in the field.
- What could you personally do better to help the support services managers be more successful in their jobs?

"OK, this is how I want to proceed today. I want to discuss *how* we can grow, but I want to always keep in mind all the elements it takes to be successful in growth. Those of us in the room today are only part of the equation. I asked you to answer four questions before the meeting, and I want to talk through them. Backward."

Everyone looked confused. Maria was enjoying this. David was, of course, the first one to ask the question.

"Why are we going to answer the questions backward? Don't we need to discuss a new structure first? And announce my promotion?" David made the last question more of a statement and made a dramatic sweep of his eyes around the room. All he received in return were groans and rolled eyes.

"No, David, we are going to start with the last question, and I think you'll understand why in just a bit."

David seemed dissatisfied, but she kept going.

"I asked each of you to describe what you could personally do better to help the support services managers be more successful in their jobs. I have your answers, but I'd like to get some dialogue going here."

The room was quiet while people looked down at the table or nervously at each other. Crickets would have been deafening in the room.

"Do you know why it is so quiet in here?"

More silence, but now some guilty looks.

"Is it because no one had any answers, only complaints of how they frustrate you?"

Some people started to meet her eyes as the full impact of this resonated through the room.

"I initially asked the four questions I did, in the order that I did, for a reason. And what I received in response had everything to do with what you each wanted *for yourself* and nothing about what you wanted for the good of the entire company."

Maria knew she was making people uncomfortable, but the change had to begin somewhere.

"Look, everyone, I'm not trying to make you feel bad, but I do need you to be aware. When I started today, I asked how you felt about me saying *the company* is stagnant. The reality of it is, a company will be stagnant if the leadership team is stagnant. I believe we are wearing blinders. After all, if we are looking out only for ourselves, doesn't that prove the point?"

Heads nodded slowly, and with looks of guilt.

"Now let me also be perfectly honest. I was no different from any of you. I was operating in the same mindset until a few weeks ago."

Maria's confession now raised some eyebrows and had more people back to looking her in the eye.

"I had been suffering from the same fear of disrupting the status quo. I am proud of what we have accomplished in the last two years. I am proud to have you all on my team. But the way we have been operating, both from a reporting structure standpoint and a sales approach standpoint, I found myself reflecting on what is lost to us when we don't grow."

A few heads began to nod in thoughtfulness now.

"I've recently been introduced to some new concepts for growth and communication in a company. I've had the privilege to spend time with a dynamic leadership team in another industry who faced huge challenges compared with the security we have been enjoying. I've seen what they were able to accomplish when they began to work together. Unless every part of the company works together, they believe that nothing can be accomplished. That is what I want for us. I want us to create a new dynamic where every part of our company focusses on the same objective. Do you see now why I wanted to start with the questions in reverse?"

The nods and murmurs of agreement were powerful. Maria saw something new in her team. She saw a new sense of responsibility and quite a bit of humility.

Roger was the first to speak. "I hear what you are saying. It is often easy to get mad at marketing, for instance, when they screw up an ad. And boy, does that happen often! I think I've always thought, 'It's me against them.' But what do they gain if my ad is wrong? Nothing. They look bad just like we do."

People couldn't argue with that logic. It would have been ridiculous to do so.

"Thank you, Roger. Tell me more though. What is even more detrimental to all of us in your example?"

"Well, I see it now. The company loses. We lose money if we must redo an ad. We lose money if the phone doesn't ring because the wrong phone number is listed. We increase our operating costs when anything goes wrong."

"Right, Roger. Is there more? What is a solution?"

"Clearly, instead of blaming another department or being frustrated, we need to work together better. If we work together better from the start, we can avoid more mistakes. I feel like I have some apologizing to do."

As this statement from Roger settled on the group, Maria went to the glass with the jelly beans and handed one to Roger, much to his confusion. She didn't explain her actions yet and instead said to Roger, "Tell me more, Roger. What would you say to the marketing team?"

"Well, I think it would be good for me to admit that I've been tough on them instead of recognizing that, even when there are mistakes, we are all on the same team. If I apologize for the times I've been cranky, maybe we can start fresh."

At that, Maria put up the slide Jane had shown with the little boy and the broken window. She was grateful that Jane let her steal some of her stuff.

"Yes, Roger. Sometimes we just have to say, 'I'm sorry.'"

People nodded, some a little ashamed and some deep in thought.

"Is this jelly bean meant to make me feel better?" Roger asked as he popped it into his mouth.

Maria laughed. "No, Roger. It is something I recently heard that I thought was very intuitive. I was with a group of people at a conference when we were talking about needing to apologize to someone. The woman who shared the idea said that when you need to apologize, you are giving something of yourself to the other person. She likened the idea of 'giving jelly beans' as a symbol of the weight of the apology."

People seemed to be grasping the idea, so she continued.

"Roger, if I needed to apologize to you and I gave you a jelly bean or two or three, I now have a bank account of jelly beans with you. Does that make sense?"

Roger nodded yes, as did others. There were a few smiles now.

"And," she said, looking back to Roger, "if I have built a bank account of jelly beans with you and I need something from you … " Roger nodded cheerfully.

"You have credit with me!" Roger smiled as he said this.

"Yes!" Maria exclaimed.

After everyone seemed to be considering this, she asked, "Does anyone else have a thought to add?"

"Where do we start then?" asked Mike. "As I said earlier, I am busier than I can imagine, and I don't have time to stop to apologize to every person in our corporate office. I would be bankrupt from buying jelly beans!"

Maria could always count on Mike to be a speed bump, but she appreciated the way he kept the theme going and his attempt at some humor.

"Mike, tell me more." Out of the corner of her eye, she saw Roger put the pieces together on her questioning strategy. A few more people seemed to begin to realize something was going on with her.

"Maria, come on," Mike said. "What are you asking of us? What do you want? It's not my fault that there are so many screw-ups in the corporate office. Can't they just do their jobs so that I can do mine? Maybe they owe *me* a few jelly beans!"

Laurie jumped in now. "Mike, I think what Maria is getting at here is that their jobs are important too. They want to get their jobs right as much as we do. But if we aren't looking at each other as teammates, then we are letting them down as much as we feel they are letting us down. Is that right, Maria?"

Maria smiled and nodded. Laurie was emerging as a gifted leader. She was the daughter of one of the original owners and had enjoyed her position because of both her family and her talent. In the last two years, Laurie had become a force all on her own. She drew the best out of her team.

"I would agree, Laurie. Mike, does that make sense?"

Mike nodded but didn't look happy about it. Maria didn't want to press him, but she was going to have to speak with him soon. His attitude was agitated and strong today. He had great potential as a leader but didn't always keep his emotions in check.

"Let me ask you all the question again. What could each of you do better to help the support services managers be more successful in their jobs?"

Answers came more rapidly as people warmed to the concept. She wrote the responses as they came and then allowed the team to review the list to see if anything was missing.

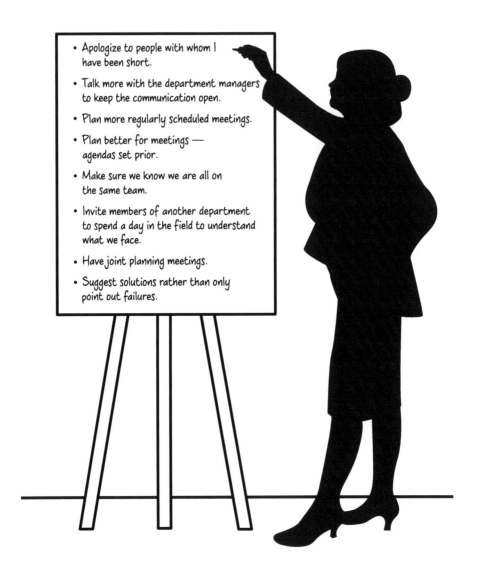

"Can anyone see anything else we are missing?" People seemed thoughtful, but it was a good start. No one seemed to have anything else to add.

"OK, then let's go to the next question. What do you need from the support services managers to be successful in your current job?"

This question received more calm responses now than it would have received before the last 10 minutes of discussion. The responses on the board were strangely similar to the responses to the previous question but fewer and more compact.

"I don't know if you all realize this, but when you sent me your responses, the laundry list of things you wanted, needed, or demanded were very specific. But the answers you just gave here are more general. Why do you think that is?"

Laurie was the first to respond this time. "Before, we were looking too closely, just at our selfish needs. I hate to say it that way, but I think it fits. Now, trying to look at these people as members of our entire team, it's a lot easier to think about strategies rather than nitpick."

"Excellent. Anyone else?"

"I guess I never thought of this before today," David interjected, "but when my wife is upset with me about something, if she has a laundry list of things that I have done that bug her, it's pretty hard to let that go to enjoy dinner, if you know what I mean." David patted his stomach and laughed, and the group laughed with him. It was a great insight, and Maria was thrilled to have his interaction like that.

"David, I hear you! That is a great example. If we spend too much time on the minute details, how do we ever move the relationship forward? And working with a large corporate team is a relationship, on both sides. After all, sometimes we in the field wake up grumpy with funny hair and bad breath. We don't want the in-house team reminding us of that, do we?"

Now people were warming up and openly chuckling at her comment, especially as she put a picture on the screen of a person with amazing bed-head hair.

Maria could feel a change beginning. *We can do this!* she thought.

As the morning went on, the team solidified a plan for working better with the corporate departments, operating from the premise that the company needed to work as one. Most of the time Maria was merely a scribe, and she was pleased that so many people showed their talents for direction and mediation with their peers. There was new energy with a focus they had not had before.

When she allowed for the morning break, Maria brought out the basket of phones, much to everyone's delight.

"All right, everyone. You have a break for 27 minutes and 42 seconds." Everyone groaned at her familiar odd timing for breaks. "As promised, you have access to your phones until we reconvene at 11:00 a.m."

People almost jumped over each other to grab their phones and power back up. Maria had to laugh, mostly because of how it reminded her of Jane's first seminar.

Promptly at 11:00 a.m., Maria got everyone settled back in and sent the basket around. Mike tried unsuccessfully to keep his hidden, but Jesse ratted him out. Everyone got a good laugh as Mike made feeble attempts to act innocent. Maria regained control while she took Mike's phone.

"Folks, we made some great strides this morning with ideas on how we can help facilitate a great working relationship with the support services departments. What I didn't tell you was that while we worked on this activity here, the managers in the corporate office were doing the same thing, led by Mark."

This elicited some interest. Maria also saw some nervous-looking glances around the room.

"That team is going to join us here for the second half of our day. After lunch, they are going to present their suggestions, and you will do the same." The team was unprepared for all the fun they were having.

"It's 11:00 a.m. now, and the support services managers should be arriving right around lunch at noon. I have an activity for you. Split yourself into four groups. You have between now and lunch to create a 10-minute presentation on how we can and will work better as one company team."

People started looking around, somewhat shocked, but already forming groups.

"Any rules? Who do you want to present?" asked David.

"There are no rules, David. You'll have to decide who presents for yourselves. I'll wander around the room if you need help. Now get started."

Maria wondered how many people would recognize that these activities were a job interview of sorts. As she wandered through the room, she watched people, looking for those who emerged as natural leaders. Although some people, like David, performed to her expectations, trying to take control by force, others surprised her.

Elaine, for instance, was sharing some interesting history on how she worked in her previous company with their corporate office. Her team seemed very engaged, and they included a few of her quotes and thoughts in their presentation.

Roger was sitting back in his group, quietly encouraging a few of the newer managers to give input. He was a great developer of talent. Two in his group were flourishing under his praise.

Not sure if she would mention it later, Maria observed how the groups operated secretly, trying to make sure the group next to them wouldn't hear their plan. She had never really thought before about how this behavior often happened when groups formed. There seemed to be a natural inclination to compete, and that was terribly at odds with what they were trying to accomplish. But the follow-up activity certainly would help them see the bigger picture.

Maria was smiling, content with their progress, when Mark came in close to lunchtime. The support services managers entered quietly, looking a little uncomfortable. As people started to head toward the room for lunch, however, she saw some interaction beginning.

"How goes the war?" he asked.

"I couldn't ask for a better day so far. How about you?"

"I would agree. We dealt in honesty all morning. Both teams are a little nervous about this meeting and excited to stand up for themselves. Are you ready for part two?"

"Oh yes. I am. We'll see if they are!" Mark and Maria smiled at their shared secret of what was to come.

Roger came up to her as she was sitting down to eat.

"Maria, *tell me more* about this strategy of yours!" he said with a smile and a wink. Maria smiled along with him.

"Seriously, Maria, this is great. I am excited. I think we have some new fun ahead of us!"

And with that, Roger ran off to grab an open seat. Maria knew that they were on the right path.

Chapter 7

THE DEFINITION OF A LEADER

Halfway through lunch, Maria put the basket with the phones on one of the tables, committed to letting people catch up on work activities before resuming the meeting. When they entered the meeting room at 1:00 p.m., people made only feeble attempts to keep their phones as the basket was passed around. Even Mike commented on how nice it was to unplug for a while.

Maria got everyone settled back into the conference room and had to laugh at how the support services managers were seated physically apart from the sales managers. It had been much the same at lunch. Even though everyone was here to start building bridges, the chasm was vast.

"All right, everyone. Thank you for joining us!" she said to the support services managers. "I understand you are all ready to present your results from your morning to us, correct?"

Heads nodded yes.

"Before we begin that exercise, however, I want to discuss a concept together as a group." Making a round of eye contact with the support services managers, Maria said, "I believe Mark brought you all up to speed on the fact that we are going to restructure the sales organization."

Heads nodded yes again, and Maria was struck again by the lack of comfort in the whole room. She had made great strides with the sales managers in the morning, but she knew this entire project wouldn't be easy.

"As we build a plan, not only for restructure of the sales organization, but also to get our company focused on growth, we will all need to be strong leaders. Our roles are vital to our success. What are your thoughts on what makes a good leader?" The question hung in the air for a moment.

Thomas, a relatively new manager to the company, raised his hand first. With bright red hair and fun, trendy glasses, Thomas never blended in. He was his own person. He also tended to rock back and forth in his chair when he spoke, making Maria wonder how his mind operated amongst that movement.

"Yes, Thomas. What are your thoughts?"

"Well, I've always believed that a good leader is dependable. And I mean not only in commitment but in their consistency."

"Interesting, Thomas. Tell me more."

"What I mean by that is that if you are a hothead one day, laughing and joking with your folks the next, and moody another day, it is distracting. People don't know what to expect. I want them to trust my word, and I want them to know that I am the same person every day."

"Very nice insight, Thomas. How do you think you do in this area?"

"Shoot! I didn't know I was going to have to rate myself!" Thomas laughed. But he seemed pleased to answer. "I know this is important to me now, and I focus on it so much, because there was a time I wasn't very good at it. When I had my first management job, I pretty much blew it. I wanted to be everyone's friend, and then that led to people not taking me seriously and taking advantage of me. When I realized what was happening, I got pretty upset and angry. I think it was hell to work for me."

Maria was very impressed by his openness and honesty and could see his colleagues, especially a few managers from the corporate office, nodding their understanding. Most managers went through the same journey at the beginning of their management careers.

"Tell me more," Maria coaxed.

"I'd like to think that now I am more even-tempered. People know that what they see is what they get, for the most part."

"Thank you, Thomas. Who else has a thought?"

Mike was, of course, next. "That is all well and good, but you can't be a pushover. A good leader has to be tough."

It took enormous willpower for Maria to keep a straight face and not make assumptions about Mike's remark.

"Interesting as well, Mike. Tell me more."

"Well, I'm not saying you have to be a jerk. I think you have to set clear expectations, so people don't walk all over you like Thomas said."

"Tell me more ... "

"I know that my people probably don't always like me, which is okay. I want them to be a little uncomfortable."

"Tell me more ... "

"Why do you keep asking that?" Mike asked with frustration. By now several more people had caught on, and those folks shared a light chuckle. Most of the support services managers looked confused.

"Why do I ask what, Mike?" Maria asked with a mischievous grin.

"Why do you keep asking me to tell you more?"

"Mike, why do *you* think I keep asking you that?"

Mike just looked at her, dumbfounded and a little irritated. He sat like that, looking perplexed, for a good 30 seconds until all of a sudden, he broke out laughing.

"You sneaky thing you!" He almost shouted through his laughter and pointed an accusing finger at her. "Here I am trying hard to play devil's advocate, and you are manipulating me into your web of change!"

Maria laughed with him. "Tell me more! Mike, why are you playing devil's advocate?"

"OK, I give," Mike said as he calmed his laughter. "I'm not trying to be difficult. I like to know I've asked every question before I accept

a new premise. It is the way I am. My family says I am overly analyt-
ical and tell me I should have been a lawyer. But mostly, I want to
fully believe in something before I embrace it. Sue me!" Mike said
with a big smile.

"Mike, I cannot thank you enough for your honesty. I think your
colleagues appreciate it too." Maria said, glancing around the room,
where people were smiling and nodding their heads, especially
a couple of support services managers whom Maria knew he went
toe-to-toe with often.

"I'll be honest. Sometimes I mistake your questions for disagree-
ment or argument. What you've just shared helps me to understand
you better. Now that I know this, I am better prepared to work with
you and help you dissect every part of any plan when you're not
completely certain. I promise to not jump to conclusions. Deal?"

"Deal!" Mike said, still grinning. "Shall I continue then?"

"Absolutely!"

"OK then, let me see if I can say this better. I don't want people to
think of me as a jerk, but sometimes I have difficulty walking that
line, a lot like Thomas was saying. I was burned early in my career too
and decided if people saw me as tough, I would be respected, maybe
a little feared," he said with a sly smile, "but people would always
know my expectations."

That made sense to Maria, and she thought the dialogue might be
helping Mike see a new potential side of himself, as well.

"But as we are talking about it, I do know that I intimidate people.
At my last company, my coworkers threw me a going-away party.
I can't tell you how many people came up to me, especially after

a cocktail or two, to tell me that although they always liked me, I was intimidating. That bothered me, but I couldn't understand what I did that made them feel that way."

"Do you have more thoughts on that now, Mike?"

"I suppose so. I am quick to answer rather than diving down on issues with people. Perhaps this 'tell me more' concept might be worth a try." Anyone who didn't get it before certainly understood now.

"Excellent, Mike. Thank you for your honesty. Would it be safe to say then that you think one quality of a good leader is being strong rather than tough and should listen as much as lead?" She was taking some liberties with his words, but it seemed a good gamble given his current state of mind.

"That sounds a lot more professional than I would have put it, but okay. I'll give you that win, Maria."

"Wonderful! Maria said with a big smile. "Who's next? I'd also like to hear from our team at the corporate office." She didn't even glance Mark's way. They had already agreed that she was now leading as CEO, teaching this team to walk as one.

"OK, I'll give my two cents," said Jeff. Jeff was the head of recruiting, a difficult job on the best of days. A smile and nod from Maria permitted him to continue.

"I think a leader has to be willing to do anything he or she asks of those they lead."

Maria nodded, and he continued.

"My team has a very challenging job. They must actively find quality people to fill our positions around the country. We are fielding through more resumes than ever, trying to give you the best candidates, and some of our positions turn over frequently."

The sales managers nodded. Everyone in the room felt the pang of panic when one of the frontline staff quit.

"We are also trying to find the best and most qualified candidates." Jeff said, "I want my team to know that I am willing to work just as hard as they do." Maria liked how he was engaging the sales team. Instead of talking and looking just at her, he was actively speaking to each of the sales managers. She knew that many of these folks gave Jeff and his team grief daily, so it probably took a lot of guts to stand up like this.

"Tell me more, Jeff. Can you give us some specific examples of what you are talking about?" Maria prompted.

"Absolutely. Each Monday at 4:00 p.m., we all stand up from our desks and meet in the middle of the room. I call it a 'stand-up' meeting. We do a stand-up every morning as well, but I want to highlight why Monday is different. We take about two minutes per person to celebrate any hires, and everyone gets the chance to discuss any open critical position they need help with."

People were nodding. They liked the idea of a daily meeting, and Maria could see some different ways to use this.

"Anyway, I pick one recruiter each Monday who is facing the most urgent open position, and every Tuesday I dedicate as much of my day as needed to either directly recruit with that person or else to take all their phone screens and other distracting work so that they can meet your urgent needs first. Sometimes that takes all my day, and sometimes not much, but whatever focus I can give them helps. If I get done quickly, I work with the next most urgent placement, et cetera. Tuesdays are my 'talent support' days if you will."

Maria was impressed. She had no idea that Jeff did this. And from the looks around the room, none of the sales managers did either.

"You do this every Tuesday?" asked Mike.

Mike followed up Jeff's 'yes' with a comment. "Jeff, I know sometimes I am on your case about getting a position filled if I think that Tammy, the recruiter for my region, isn't moving on it fast enough."

Jeff nodded his agreement, and Mike looked a little guilty. "I had no idea you did this, Jeff. Thank you for being that dedicated to our needs. I promise to be a better team member from here on out with both you and Tammy."

"Deal!" Jeff smiled. "Look, Mike, I get it. When you are short-staffed, it makes it hard to do your job. We know that, and we are all working as hard as we can. Unfortunately, sometimes things don't come together as fast as we would like."

"Yep," said Mike. "I have a saying. 'No one's sense of urgency ever matches my own.'"

Maria loved this. She snuck a glance at Mark, and he gave her a slight nod to acknowledge that he too was pleased with the progress they were making.

"Maria," Mike called her attention back.

"Yes?"

"Can you please give Jeff a jelly bean for me?" All the sales managers got a good chuckle, and the support services managers looked confused. Mike simply looked at Jeff and said, "I'll explain it at the break, man. Suffice it to say, I am in your debt."

Jeff nodded and smiled, and Maria continued.

"Jeff, thank you for sharing your story. I can see that the entire sales team was impressed." Everyone nodded all around the room, and the murmurs were positive and filled with genuine appreciation and admiration. Maria continued to ask him, "Is there anything the sales managers can do to help you and your team?"

At this question, everyone seemed to lean forward in their chairs.

"Well, I suppose there are a few things. First, remind your staff that they can help us by recommending people they know would be great additions. Even if we don't have a spot for someone now, we love to have a pool of qualified candidates. And they should enjoy the referral bonus when someone they recommended gets hired. We've been slacking in direct referrals from our staff lately."

Maria could see her team taking notes.

"Also, make sure to take some time to get to know your recruiter. If you're in the corporate office, don't forget to stop by and say hello to the whole team. I know we are a little out of the way on the second floor of the building. We sit apart because we deal with highly sensitive information. But that privacy also sometimes makes us invisible."

Maria found herself nodding along with the sales team, clearly recognizing how this group gets overlooked. And yet the role they play is vital.

"And it would be great to have one or two of you share with the entire recruiting team an overview of what you look for in a candidate. Maybe we could even have our recruiters spend a day in a store?" Jeff asked, turning toward Maria.

"Absolutely, Jeff!" Everyone nodded enthusiastically. "I think that is a great idea!"

"I have another suggestion," Jesse piped up, his drawl drawing everyone's attention. "Candice is my recruiter. Last month I invited her to listen in while I did a phone screen with someone she had sent to me. I think she got a lot out of the call. She was on mute, but I wanted her to hear the questions I ask a potential sales rep before I agree to meet them in person."

"I remember that!" Jeff jumped in. "She was excited, and the other recruiters were jealous that they couldn't listen in. I bet there are quite a few creative things we could do!"

People were excited now. In talking about leadership, they were already also moving toward genuinely beneficial relationships.

"Jeff, thank you for all of that," Maria said, getting people focused again. "I think we can all agree that there are many exciting opportunities for all of us to work better together." Heads nodded briskly in agreement.

"And all those ideas stemmed from the initial question of what it takes to be a leader. Before we move on, does anyone else have a leadership trait you think we should discuss?"

This time Dennis spoke up. Dennis had the potential to be a great sales leader. He had years of experience selling in some of the stores he now managed, but he seemed to struggle with the balance between being a friend and a leader. On more than one occasion, Maria had to help him refocus and set his priorities. She wanted him to succeed, but now it was up to him.

"I think we also need to have a little fun. I want people to enjoy coming to work."

People all around the room murmured agreement. Maria felt it was good insight, but still not where he needed to focus. At least it was a start, however.

"Tell me more, Dennis."

"Well, we are all working really hard. I've known most of my team since I was selling alongside them. These are good people who feel stressed. Maybe we should go bowling once a month or something."

"OK, Dennis, let me ask you this. Do you think an activity at work makes work fun, or are there other ways we can also make work enjoyable?"

Dennis looked somewhat confused.

"Let me tell you what I mean by that, Dennis. I have no problem with us doing team-building activities into our regions when appropriate. I think that is great for everyone. But I want to make sure we are clear about whether we want people to enjoy their work because we allow them fun activities once or twice a year or because we are helping them master their job and feel more confident in themselves. What are your thoughts?"

Dennis didn't quite look confident in an answer, and Roger jumped in with an answer.

"I think that the more we empower our teams, the more they will enjoy their work anyway. An activity would be icing, and we should celebrate together from time-to-time, but I think what you are getting at is that an employee who feels valued and empowered will be happier with their job."

People around the room nodded to this.

"Roger, that is exactly what I am going for. Dennis, does that make sense?"

"Yeah, I do. Maybe sometimes I want to be a friend, and what I need is to be more of a leader."

Maria couldn't help her smile of relief. *We'll see if it sticks with him,* she thought. But at least it was an admission in front of his peers.

For the next 30 minutes, the team worked together to develop their list of the traits of a good leader, and Maria put them on the flipchart as they went along.

Once the group was confident in the list, Maria was ready to take them to the next level.

Maria advanced to the next slide.

People looked confused, just as Maria had planned.

"I bet you are all wondering what this means," Maria said. People nodded around the room.

"As I told the sales managers earlier today, I've been introduced to some new ways to approach our business. I had the chance to sit with a team of very talented folks who had to come together as a group like we are doing here today." Maria looked around the room to make sure people were with her.

"I sat in on the senior leadership meeting of Home Away, a national long-term care company. Three years ago, those managers were operating much as we have been," Maria said, looking people in the eye. "They were operating in silos of their respective jobs and departments. And the company was in trouble."

It was satisfying to see people appear interested in where she was going.

"No matter their position or department, these managers decided together that they would have a common goal. Census equates to patients in beds, so you can consider 100 percent census as every bed filled." People nodded and were following along, starting to understand.

"Today they operate as one team, knowing that the panacea of their efforts will mean every bed filled, every day, in every building around the country." Maria let that sit, quietly waiting for the impact of the goal to hit them as it had hit her.

"Wait!" David said, making Maria smile as she had anticipated him as being the first voice to question. "How is that even possible? I mean, I guess it is possible, but it's not probable."

Before Maria had the chance to say it, Mike jumped in, "Tell me more, David!" Even David had to laugh at that.

When he looked eager to continue, Maria nodded to Mike, who took that as permission to give his thoughts.

"I bet I see where you are going with this, Maria. And, David," he said, nodding David's way, "I would have said the same thing you did before today. Now I think I get it. The Home Away managers figured that even though it might seem improbable to reach that goal, it was still possible. But *only* if they all worked together as one team."

Maria was beaming with pride. She couldn't help it. As she looked around the room, she could see everyone buying in, starting to look at their jobs and their mission from a different viewpoint.

"Mike, I couldn't have said it better myself," Maria said, and Mike, uncharacteristically, beamed from the acknowledgment.

"What I want," Maria continued, "is for us to come up with our common mission. How can we make sure that we set a target for ourselves that is possible, even if it doesn't seem probable?"

"We need to focus it on our customers," added Jesse, getting approving nods from the room.

"Maybe we need to talk about almost a mission statement for us as a leadership team, not just the one we have hanging on the walls of our stores," Gracie offered.

After some heated discussion, they at least had a working platform. Maria wrote the first draft of their mission statement on the board:

Promote vision health in every community we serve. Ensure that all customers purchase appropriate eyewear on their first visit and are satisfied to stay with us for life.

"What do you think, folks?" Maria asked. "We can still play with it in the next few weeks until we are all satisfied." The group seemed happy to have some time to let it simmer.

Maria allowed the group a brief break, 9 minutes and 32 seconds to be exact. She loved giving break times that were odd and unusual, and Dennis gave her a nod to show he saw this as one way to interject some fun into their day. Strangely, not one person requested their phone at the break.

Chapter 8

BEING PUT THROUGH THE WRINGER

After the break, Maria called the group back to order. As everyone got settled, Maria continued.

"If you've noticed, I've gone through some unusual activities in our agenda so far today."

"No kidding!" said David. "My head is spinning!" Everyone got a little chuckle, probably because they all felt it.

"I'm sure it is, David, and it will keep spinning. Let me recap so far what we've discussed. First, we started the day by forcing you all to admit that the company has been stagnant and that we all have blinders on. There is nothing like starting a fresh day with insults, right?"

People were able to laugh, now that a little time had passed.

"No," interrupted Jesse, "first, you cut off our arms when you took away our phones!"

"Jesse, you are right!" laughed Maria. "I forced you all to *listen* to me while I insulted you!" People enjoyed that line.

"Then I called you all selfish and made you talk about playing nice with the support services team, and they got the same treatment back with Mark."

Everyone in the room smiled, especially the support services managers.

"That wasn't so bad," added Laurie. "We needed to hear that, and I think our solutions are great, especially the ones we keep adding together."

"I do too, Laurie," Maria agreed. "I think they will go a long way towards us becoming a fully-integrated company."

"Then I surprised you all, giving you virtually no warning that all the amends we need to make with each other, both field and support services, begin today," Maria continued.

"And I think we still need some time to work on our presentations," added David.

"Don't worry, David," said Maria. "You'll have a chance."

Mollified, he nodded his approval.

"Then we talked about traits of a good leader, which provided Mike with a free therapy session."

"Yeah," Mike added. "Only 99 more to go and I'll be cured!"

"Good luck with that," David said. Mike promptly threw a piece of candy at David.

"Does anyone have an idea why I wanted to discuss the traits of a good leader before our presentations and before discussing a new organizational structure?"

Although everyone contributed to the discussion throughout the day, Maria was pleased to have Gracie speak up. Gracie was a fun mix of true intelligence, witty banter, and serious business. She often referred to herself in the third person as "that cool chick." Maria enjoyed her and always welcomed her frankness.

"Well, if I am picking up everything you're laying down today, I would say that you want to make sure we fully understand what it takes to be a leader during the change. I imagine it takes a different skill set from being a leader in a 'stagnant' company." The air quotes and the slant to her head indicated that she really did believe, but she wanted to poke some fun at Maria's sneaky methods. Gracie also said this all with a sly smile and a slow wink at the end, making it hard for Maria to keep a straight face.

"Tell me more, Gracie. You're on the right track."

"Well," Gracie said, leaning back in her chair and taking a moment of drama to make sure everyone was listening, "I would assume that part of today is also a type of interview. Who among us can rise to a position of leadership over their peers?"

Wow, thought Maria, *I can't fool her at all.*

People around the room sat up a little more as the thought took root.

"Very interesting, Gracie. What do you think I'm looking for?"

"The way I see it," Gracie began, clearly enjoying what she had realized before her peers, "you're going to have to add a layer of management if you are going to keep from having all of us yahoos reporting directly to you. Someone who takes a position like that will have to be solid and believe in all the things we are covering today. I have a sneaky suspicion that you are watching us very closely." Gracie finished this statement with a waving finger at Maria and a smile.

"You're right on many levels, Gracie," Maria agreed, smiling. "By focusing on the traits of a good leader, it is a good reminder for us all of what we should all expect of ourselves and each other. And in this room, we have a group of talented people who bring a lot to the table. We need to be on the same page. I expect it of you all as leaders."

As she looked around the room, people were thoughtful. She had been concerned that some of the sales managers would be worried or try to start to position themselves for promotion. But what she saw instead was a group of people genuinely embracing that change in a stagnant company was going to take more than just a new reporting structure. It had to start with attitude.

"Does this make sense to everyone?" Heads nodded slowly while they still contemplated all she and Gracie had said.

"So, presenting to the support services managers," Jesse said then, drawing everyone's focus, "is not just about presenting what we discussed, is it? You want to make sure that change starts with us today. Right?"

"Exactly, Jesse. That is it exactly. Do you all see it?"

Now people understood the magnitude of what needed to happen. Heads nodded slowly but purposefully.

"In that case," David said, "can we *please* have a bit more time to prepare?" Several voices leaned their agreement.

"Absolutely. But I am going to shake things up a bit." With this statement, some managers from the sales team audibly groaned, and the corporate team looked apprehensive.

"Mark, you have divided the support services managers into two groups?"

"Yep. They are ready." He looked so proud of them.

"OK, so this is what is going to happen now. Our sales managers divided into four groups because of how many there are. To make this a little fairer" — Maria let that hang for a moment to build some suspense — "I think it's only right that the sales managers regroup into two groups."

"What?"

"How?"

"We just got our presentations down!"

Maria gave a sideways glance at Mark, who was trying very hard not to laugh.

"I realize that folks, but to be fair to our guests here, I need you to regroup, making just two groups."

People looked confused and flustered.

"And" — now people were looking back to her again — "you'll each invite one of the support services teams to join you. Instead of presenting to each other, field to corporate, you will be two larger groups presenting a united front to the other group."

Everyone seemed baffled, but that didn't deter Maria.

"You have 15 minutes to get your presentations organized and united. Go!"

Several people sat stunned for a few seconds, unable to move. Others jumped right up and started making connections. Mark and Maria sat far away from everyone, just watching. Whenever anyone would ask a question to either of them, they would respond, "What do you think you should do?"

Mark leaned into her, whispering, "Goodness, Maria, I haven't had this much fun in a long time! Makes me wish, *almost*, that I wasn't ready to retire!"

When Maria gave the 5-minute warning, the noise and stress level went up in the room. She knew she was putting them through something they had not expected. She hoped the gamble paid off.

At 3:15 p.m., Maria stood up again and had to whistle to get everyone's attention.

"OK, folks, please be seated." After a few minutes of chair dragging, everyone settled down.

"Now, before you give your presentations, let me ask you a few questions. First, how did each of you form your original groups?"

This question threw everyone off. They were mentally ready to present, even if they weren't entirely prepared.

Jesse spoke first. "I think my group just kind of gravitated together. We have worked together for a long time and know each other. We needed a few more people to make the groups even, so a couple of people on our team stole Elaine and Kelly."

"Thank you, Jesse. But let me ask you a question."

Jesse looked ready for anything she could throw at him; he was always calm.

"Why did you feel the need to keep the groups equal in size?"

The usually cool and calm Jesse opened his mouth slightly to answer, but nothing came out.

"Anyone?" Maria asked.

"Um, well, we thought that was what you wanted," answered David.

"Did I specify four groups of equal size?" Maria asked.

Everyone was flabbergasted.

After a few seconds with no other responses, Maria gave them all an out.

"Can we all agree that you 'assumed' I meant you to form groups of equal size?" Heads nodded in agreement.

"Can we also all agree that you all operated from a 'like it always is' mentality? I mean, after all, most times when you do an exercise like Mark and I put you through, you would form equal-sized groups, correct?" Heads nodded again, and a few people began to ponder the lesson here.

"So what lesson do you think I am trying to teach by asking you why you assumed groups of equal size?"

Janet, the VP of marketing, spoke up. "Well, it seems to me that if our primary objective here today is to get the corporate and field leadership team acting as one, we better not operate the way we always have in the past."

"Yes, Janet, that is great. Tell me more."

"I suppose it is the definition of insanity. When I think about how we formed our groups at corporate, without even thinking about what we were doing, it looks like we grouped with departments that are physically close to each other in the office. Marketing, the call center, and HR are all in the same part of the building. Finance and operations are on the other. It looks like we just grouped naturally with the departments close to us."

Her colleagues nodded in agreement and seemed surprised as well.

"Thank you, Janet. Tell me more. What do you think about how you did that now that we are looking at it from a different perspective?"

"It's yet another version of insanity, I guess. If we tend to gravitate to the same groups whether it is because we work together often or work in the same proximity, how will we generate new paths, new ideas?" People seemed to be warming to the concept. "Change is about looking at what you do naturally and questioning it, I suppose."

"I like that idea," Maria said. "Does anyone else have input on how you decided on your groups?"

There was quiet.

"OK, how did you decide *what* to present?" She kept the conversation going.

"We based most everything on the lists we developed earlier today," said Elaine. "It was pretty much all laid out for us."

"Thank you, Elaine. But I noticed that you were sharing some other things with your group. Can you tell us more about that?"

"Sure. The more I thought about our lists from this morning, the more I remembered things from my last company. Our field managers had excellent relationships with the support services managers. We all seemed to work well together, so I shared some of the things we did to keep that going."

"Like what? Can you give us a real-life example?"

"Yes. You know how we all decided this morning that we should have a support services manager spend a day in the field to see what we do? And like what we discussed before the break with Jeff and his recruiting team?"

Maria nodded her agreement.

"Well, in my old company, we would have each new manager spend one full day with each department before they went into the field, and then we did that once a year on the manager's anniversary month. It took people out of the field for five days a year, which some people struggled with, but it improved their relationships and understanding of the other departments."

"And" — Maria nodded for Elaine to continue — "now that I look back, I see something. The managers who embraced those days were the best in the company. They went in ready to learn and experience.

The managers who dreaded those days and complained about them were not as successful as their colleagues. They weren't as well-respected by their teams or the corporate staff."

"Thank you, Elaine. Excellent. Why do you think those managers were the most successful?"

"I know for me it was because it allowed me to get to know people personally. When your corporate office is 2,000 miles away, and most of your contact with those folks is by phone or email, it is challenging to remember you are dealing with a person."

Maria nodded her agreement, and Elaine continued. *I think this day is doing wonders for her self-confidence!*

"And on those days that I spent with the corporate staff, I came prepared with questions I wouldn't usually ask. For instance, in dealing with marketing, to Roger's point earlier, when there is a mistake, you tend to focus on the error.

"My first day with the marketing team on my first anniversary, I asked if I could sit with the proofreader for my region. I wanted to see what she had to face. When I saw the sheer volume of what she had to do every day, I was floored. It gave me a new appreciation for her. Together we found a way for me to rotate some of my team to help her with one last set of eyes before every piece went out. Then if there was a problem, she wasn't the only person who felt the burden. From that point on, I tried to look at solutions, not be sidetracked by problems. You have to see the problems to find solutions, but you can control how much of your energy is wrapped up in the problems."

Maria saw Janet making notes and could already see another new potential bridge between the field and marketing.

"It allowed my frontline salespeople to develop trust in marketing."
Elaine continued, "They now had skin in the game when before it was
much easier to blame."

"That is fantastic, Elaine. I can see how much your insight is sparking
creativity in this room already. Does anyone else have anything
to add about how you decided on the material to present?" Maria
followed up.

"We do," said David.

At Maria's urging, he continued, "We started out with the basic lists
each group had, but then Candy from HR came up with a great idea."

Candy smiled at the compliment, but she urged David to
speak for her.

"Candy builds on what Elaine was talking about, and that is training.
Do we train everyone in our company, at every level, to know
and understand what each department does? In other words, if
I started tomorrow as a sales specialist in Ohio, would I know what
the marketing department does? Would I know how long it takes
to get an ad out and how to respond to people who call in because
of that ad?"

People were right along with David, and Maria was impressed with
this idea. "Tell me more, David."

"Well, as sales leaders, we know that when an ad drops that we
don't know is coming, it causes confusion. It might offer a certain
discount that is out of our norm, or promotes a product we don't have
in stock. Our frontline staff goes nuts, right?"

Everyone nodded in agreement.

"Right. Everyone wants to know what it means, and how it impacts recommended pricing, discounts, their commissions — everything. There is just confusion." David looked at his colleagues, and they were all with him.

"So as managers, we get the calls from freaked-out stores, and in turn, we pick up the phone and call marketing to demand to know why they put out that ad without telling us. Sorry, Janet." David nodded her way, and she gave a nod of appreciation to the admission.

"What if, instead, we not only know what ad is coming out when but work with marketing *before* the ad drops so we can *proactively* prepare our stores? That way, they are prepared for how to best sell to customers who respond to those ads!"

"Tell me more, David," Maria prompted. "Tell me exactly what this would look like."

"Okay, imagine this. Janet's team comes out with a super new ad, based on buy-one, get-one-free prescription sunglasses, for lenses and frames only, all standard. Together we write up an operating manual of sorts for this ad. Nothing too cumbersome, just a one-pager, but a tool to help us master return on investment ("ROI") on the ad."

People were leaning forward, urging David along. Maria didn't even have to encourage him. He was on a roll.

"So, the instructions might be something like this. First, schedule the customer for a full eye exam. Second, ask the patient to bring their current prescription glasses, regular or sunglasses. That way, we can see for ourselves the state their glasses are in and get an idea of what they bought, which can give you a guestimate of the amount they spent and their sense of style. Third, during the exam, make sure we ask questions about their lifestyle. If they like to fish, we promote the upgrade to polarized lenses for sure, for example."

Everyone was so excited as David continued. Janet and her two marketing managers were writing notes like crazy.

"I think we worry about what the ad says instead of wondering why the person called, understanding what the implications of that mean for the sale at the end. If we plan this better and work as a team, we can make every store in the US ready to go with a one-page quick-selling guide. I bet our ROI goes up significantly!"

David finished his statement with a flourish and enjoyed the positive responses he was getting from his colleagues.

"David, that is excellent!" Maria exclaimed.

"We came up with other department-related topics, as well, but couldn't get through too many in the short time we had. We'd like to work on it some more." David said. Maria hadn't seen him so excited in a long time. The man wanted to work!

Everyone agreed they wanted additional time together. The energy was electric in the room.

"Okay, so let me ask you all this. If instead of presenting right now, you had more time in these larger groups to compile your recommendations, would you like that?"

Everyone was excited now, verbally agreeing and nodding heads.

"OK, then let's do this. It's almost 3:45 p.m. How much time do you need so that we can still have both groups present before we break at 5:30 p.m.?"

"How about 45 minutes?" came Mike. "That way, we have 30 minutes per group to present."

People seemed to like this idea.

"I need one person from each group to keep an eye on the clock and keep your team on-time. They will also let me know when the groups are finished. Time management is your responsibility. I leave it up to you all to make sure we can accomplish everything we need to before 5:30 p.m."

And with that, people were already moving, with one group staying in the main room and the other group moving into the room where they had lunch. Maria made note that they did so this time, not so much out of secrecy, but because their energy was so high that the volume was too much for one room.

When they reconvened at 4:30 p.m., Maria and Mark were amazed by both groups presentations, and how everyone was fully involved and engaged. In the end, the suggestions on how best both field and corporate departments could work together were about so much more than ideas. They came up with strategies that pulled-in every person in the organization and would give the company a better sense of inclusion than Maria ever considered.

She stood before them, barely past the 5:30 p.m. stopping point. "Folks, you all should be very proud of what you have accomplished today. You were creative and open, and truly worked together like one team with one purpose."

People were smiling at the praise and genuinely pleased.

"Wait!" said Dennis. Maria turned to him. "I like that! One team, one purpose!"

People were nodding and agreeing. Maria loved it. "Great idea, Dennis! Tomorrow we'll include that in our mission." Dennis looked pleased to have his contribution be so well received.

"Before we break for dinner," Maria added, "I want to share something with you."

People looked interested even though were as tired as she was. It was amazing how exhausted you could be after sitting in a meeting room all day.

"Earlier this month, I developed this list of the three key objectives I want us to accomplish for this coming year. I think we made some incredible progress on this list today. What are your thoughts?"

Maria put her objectives up on the screen.

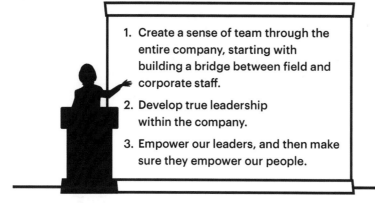

People were smiling as they read, and Maria could see a sense of swelling pride.

"I think we made incredible progress on several parts of this today!" Jesse was practically beaming as he spoke; his Southern drawl almost a purr. "I mean look at us! I'm not sure what the corporate team went through this morning, but we had a lot of tough realizations and had to admit how we were letting you guys down."

Janet was the first to speak up. "Jesse, we went through the same thing. This morning was tough for us as well, but then this afternoon it became so clear. None of us are going to be successful if we allow any part of the company to falter, especially if we are doing so to prove a point or boost our ego."

Dennis chimed in, surprising Maria yet again. "I think the last point you have up there is one I am most guilty of not doing. It is so easy to say, '*They* screwed this up,' or 'You have to do this because *they* are telling us to.' Sometimes I think my sales experience in the stores I now manage is a detriment. After all, I was in their shoes before, and it is easier to make an issue about *they* rather than about us. I think that gets in the way of people's confidence with the company."

"Dennis, that is great insight," said Maria. "What will you change when you are back in your region on Friday?"

"I need to apologize. I need to fess up to the fact I wanted to be their friend more than their boss, but by doing so, I am hurting them. I am not sure how to do that yet, but I know it's the right path. I'll be handing out a lot of jelly beans in my future."

Maria quickly flipped back to the slide with the boy who had just broken the window.

"Dennis, I bet that the next couple of days will help you decide what to do, and your colleagues and I are here to help give some insight. The important part now is that you had a great realization. What you do with that now makes all the difference."

As Maria turned back to the group, she saw that Dennis had voiced something that many were feeling, and she knew people would do a lot of thinking in the days and weeks to come.

"Let me wrap things up for today. Today was all about your ability to look at a problem from a different perspective, in a different light, and being forced to continually 'tell me more.' From that, you came to your own decisions and conclusions. And based on what both groups just presented, we made incredible progress."

People let this sink in, and Maria put one more slide on the screen for the day.

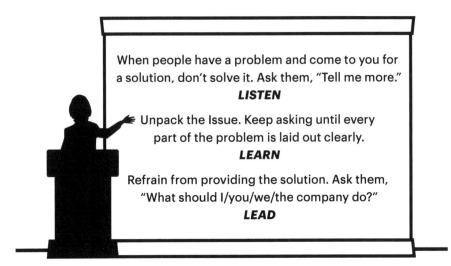

When people have a problem and come to you for a solution, don't solve it. Ask them, "Tell me more."
LISTEN

Unpack the Issue. Keep asking until every part of the problem is laid out clearly.
LEARN

Refrain from providing the solution. Ask them, "What should I/you/we/the company do?"
LEAD

Mike was the first to speak. "Maria, even though I was irritated when you were grilling me this morning, I get it now. And frankly, it makes me feel like you genuinely want to hear my thoughts. I'm not sure how good I'll be at it in the beginning, but I'm game."

"Thank you, Mike. I do care about what all of you have to say. I will give guidance when or if we are off track, but you've all already proven to me that you can come up with even greater ideas and plans than I could have just on my own. Let's build this together!"

After the cheers died down, Maria added, "Now, for our final activity tonight, let's have some fun and enjoy some time with each other. We will meet in the lobby at 6:30 p.m. and walk to the Fairmount neighborhood. We'll have a casual dinner in a restaurant with Ping-Pong and pool tables, lots of games, and even two lanes of bowling. Jeans are welcome, and the walk is only about four blocks."

People were jazzed to go. As they dispersed, she had to call a few people back to remind them to pick-up their phones!

Chapter 9

BUILDING BLOCKS

Dinner was fun for the entire team. Everyone was relaxed, laughing and interacting with people they didn't know well. Someone organized a Ping-Pong tournament, and even Maria joined in. She surprised more than a few people with her mad table tennis skills!

Nearly everyone stayed until the end, walking back to the hotel together and keeping the camaraderie alive. Maria overheard David and Janet working on a pilot for his idea to prep his teams for an upcoming ad.

As people gathered the next morning, Maria was pleased to see that people sat in different spots, better mixing support services and sales managers. People dropped their phones in the basket without being prompted, and no computers littered the tables.

"Yesterday, we ended with plans for how we can and will work better together, and that was just the beginning. I want you to keep this spirit alive, which requires us to banish one sentence from our vocabulary." She enjoyed the looks of interest and confusion.

"I no longer want to hear, 'But we've always done it that way.'" The way she mimicked a whiny voice started the day with laughter.

"I no longer want to hear, 'But we've always done it that way.'"

"We also started a list of traits of what makes a great leader and discussed what that means for all of us. We all have a responsibility here to be the type of leaders that we detailed yesterday. Would you agree?" All heads nodded. Everyone was taking this seriously and showed Maria they were on board just by their attention and energy.

"What do you think I want to discuss next?"

David jumped right in. "Well, if we are going to continue discussing our four initial homework questions, the next is, 'What do you think is the best role for you to play in this new structure, and why?' But how can we answer that if we don't know what the new structure is?"

Heads nodded. Maria was enjoying this all perhaps too much.

"Tell me more, David. Why do you think I want to discuss this question *before* determining a new structure?"

"Hmmm ... If I'm going to avoid my usual response of being so fabulous that you can't decide which job is best for me," David said, gaining him rolled eyes from around the room, "then my thought is that you *do* want our input on what the structure should look like, and you want to have us build on what we *need* as a company, instead of just what we want for ourselves."

Maria was almost speechless. Even though he still inserted his comedy, he hit the nail squarely on the head. People in the room seemed just as stunned. Who knew David had so much insight hidden under layers of bravado?

"David, that is an excellent answer." He beamed from the praise, reminding Maria that no matter the face people put on, they still want to be heard and seen.

"That is exactly what I wanted everyone to realize. Today is about preparing us for growth and understanding the pieces of the puzzle it takes to make growth successful, especially in as large of an organization as ours. Once we have the puzzle pieces on the table, we can begin to build the framework."

Jesse interjected. "Maria, I need to be honest. I've never been asked to do anything like this before. I'm not sure where we even start. It was a lot easier when I was thinking about my selfish piece of the puzzle." He smiled. That description was catching on. "How do we know if we are doing this right?"

"Great question, Jesse. What are you afraid of? Tell ... "

"Me more!" came the response from about half of the people in the room.

Jesse chuckled. "Well, I have always been successful in my region. I have a great team, and I've always had the latitude and freedom to do what I needed to do my job. But that is just my little corner of the world. You're asking us to plan a strategy for the entire company. I guess I just figured that was your job, and I will do what I need to."

Maria could see that Jesse wasn't complaining. He was trying to find a path for himself. Others slightly nodded as he spoke.

"Jesse, I appreciate your honesty. You have been very successful throughout the years. Keep with me here. *Why* do you think I want your participation in this? *Why* am I taking us through this exercise today?"

"What? No 'tell me more?'" Jesse asked with a laugh.

"I thought I might be overdoing that phrase already this morning," replied Maria, giving a sly smile. "So, I am asking the same question in a slightly different manner. What are your thoughts?"

"Well, as David said, I believe it is because you want our input. But more than that, maybe you *need* our input."

Maria signaled him to continue, giving a nonverbal form of "tell me more."

"I know that when I have an issue or want to brainstorm, I like to call you. We have great discussions, and your insight helps me. I suppose I'd like to believe that you value me, and all of us, in the same way."

Maria smiled and nodded and urged him to keep going.

"I suppose, as well, if we are a part of the planning and discussion, we will each be more committed to the process."

Maria addressed the entire room. "Would the rest of you agree with Jesse?"

Heads nodded approval of the concept.

"On the flip side, if I would have come in here this morning with my entire new strategy laid out, and spent this morning telling you exactly what I planned to do with a plan that you were not allowed any say in or to give input, how would you have all felt about that?"

"I would have probably wanted to fight you on every point," chimed in Mike with a smile. "I would have done whatever you asked me though. I know when I need to follow orders."

"I know that, Mike. But what would the fighting have done to your confidence about the plan?"

"Well, I told you earlier. I like to go through every potential downside to something before I embrace it. I am not certain what your plan would entail, so I can't comment on that, but initially, I would probably put up a lot of roadblocks just because I would want to dissect it. Or, to use your verbiage, I'd want to unpack it."

"OK, fair enough. Anyone else?"

Kelly spoke up, sharing a similar concern she had initially expressed on the conference call several weeks ago. "Honestly, as I said before, I would be nervous even if there was no valid reason to be so. My history says that restructuring equals loss of jobs. But as we've gone through this meeting the way we have, I am feeling much more confident and excited. There is still some trepidation, but it isn't fear."

"Wonderful, Kelly. Does anyone have anything different to add?"

"Well, if I can be honest," Roger said.

"Of course, you can! Please!"

"I used to own the business long before we consolidated into EyeSeeYou. And until you came here, Maria, I pretty much still operated my region the way I wanted to. Although most of you don't know this, I am pretty certain Maria wanted to strangle me a few times when we first met." He gave Maria a shrug and a smile as if to say, "Look how adorable I am."

"Roger, there is no one quite like you. Once you realized I wasn't out to get you," Maria started.

"And once I knew you were pretty good at your job," Roger added, "I have embraced all the things we've done. But if I'm sincere, a company restructure without any input from me would have felt somewhat insulting."

Maria nodded. It was a fair statement.

"Don't get me wrong. I wouldn't fight unless I felt there was input I needed to give, but I've been doing this for a long time and was there at the beginning of this company. I love what we are doing here today because it feels respectful of all of us."

People nodded to this around the room.

"Any other thoughts?" Heads shook no, so Maria continued.

"So, you all understand a little more what I'm trying to do here today?"

Heads nodded again. She was getting used to a lot of head nodding!

"Don't get me wrong. I can't have everything we do in the company come down to a democratic vote with all 40 of you. And I do have a clear vision of what we should look like as a company. But every step we took yesterday and each we take together today should help everyone to have input, get comfortable with what we decide, and launch us into the future."

The rest of the day was indeed a group-planning session. Maria could tell that, at first, the support services managers weren't sure they were needed or belonged there. After all, most of the discussion was about the new reporting structure. At first glance, it didn't seem to affect them.

As the day progressed, each of those managers began to have input and suggestions on how the new structure, or perhaps amendments to the structure, could both support and benefit from the corporate team. Janet, for instance, saw great opportunities for better marketing communications to large segments of the country rather than having one-on-one meetings with 30 different field managers.

In the end, they all accepted and agreed to the new structure. It looked precisely like Maria had envisioned, with six segments of the United States led by a sales director. Maria knew that some of the field managers would struggle with an extra layer in the reporting structure, but they couldn't argue against the necessity.

True to his word, Mark had remained quiet through the meeting, only interjecting when prompted. Although people watched him at times the first day, they seemed to accept her fully into the role in which she was transitioning.

At the end of the day, Maria pulled the focus back to what they had accomplished and went through a brief review of all that they had agreed.

"I am going to schedule a conference call for all of us in two weeks. I want to see what you have done with the things we've covered here and will be looking for examples of how we are all working better together as a leadership team." People liked that idea, and Maria knew it would help keep them all aligned with their commitments.

"And I am going to open up the sales director positions on Monday. We will see who our internal candidates are first and plan to have positions filled by February 1st." A few people made notes in their notebooks, and Maria assumed they were people who wanted to apply. "Let's get back out there, and as Dennis described, be 'One Team, One Purpose!'"

As everyone made their good-byes and headed out to the airport, Maria finally sat down. Mark came and joined her after the last person had left. He brought her a cup of coffee that was more than a little bitter after sitting all day but welcome nonetheless.

"Maria, you have been a great addition to this company, and I can't think of anyone better to take my place. I am so proud of what you took these people through the last two days. We need to start transitioning the corporate department managers to you right away. They are all eager to work with you after this meeting."

Maria smiled at the praise and felt herself blush a little. She craved his respect and felt a swell of pride in his approval.

"Mark, thank you so much. I must say, I'm a little proud of myself. I knew I wanted this role, but until today, I'm not sure I believed I was fully ready for it."

"Tell me more!" Mark queried, with a mischievous smile. Maria couldn't help but laugh along. It seemed like there was so much more laughter in her work days recently.

"I think it comes down to this. Everyone has nagging fears and doubts in the back of their mind. I've always been a very positive person, and I have been very successful, so those doubts never really control me. But taking the helm of a ship you built, and being someone I admire so much, I have to be honest that there was a little doubt back there that I could gain the full trust and support of a company that has only known you as their CEO."

"And now?" Mark prodded.

"After these last two days, I see that I empowered the team and they trust me more for that. In trying to teach them the strategy of 'tell me more,' I proved it to myself. Funny, huh? I thought I believed it to begin with."

"Maria, you *did* believe it. But it's like a circle. You can hear an idea and think, *'that makes sense,'* and believe it could work. Only when you try it yourself and *see* that it works do you more fully feel it. The real success, however, in your own belief is when you share it with others and it works for them."

Maria quietly sat quietly as she internalized just what Mark had said. She had gone on a journey the last month. She wondered what was in store for her next.

Chapter 10

THE PUDDING IS THE PROOF

About a week after the meeting, Elaine called out-of-the-blue, her voice brimming with excitement.

"Maria, do you have a minute?" Elaine asked.

"Absolutely. What's up?"

"I need to share something with you. After we left the meeting, I kept thinking about how powerful it is to say '*tell me more*' when someone comes at you with a problem or a crisis."

"Yes," Maria encouraged.

"Well, I just left our Provo store where my lead salesperson has been struggling. I couldn't figure out why her numbers were so low the last few weeks, and I wanted to spend some time there. I dedicated this whole week to them."

"OK," Maria said. "Tell me more!" Both women laughed.

"I ended up taking Shelly to lunch on Monday. She seemed stressed that I was there. She reminded me of how I must have sounded to you before you came out to ride with me last month. I was certain I was in trouble, and Shelly was feeling the same way." Maria was proud to have Elaine make the admission. It proved that she was becoming more self-aware.

"Go on," Maria prompted.

"I told her I wanted to help her and that I value her. I asked her to tell me what she thought was happening with her sales, and as she started talking, I just listened except for when I would ask her to tell me more."

"Well," Elaine continued, "she talked about frustration with the new ads and felt that they were bringing people in who were window-shopping and weren't interested in buying. When she finally got to the real heart of the issue, she admitted that she was feeling like an order-taker. She wasn't feeling challenged in her job."

"I can see that with Shelly," Maria said. "She likes to be the person other people follow."

"Yes!" Elaine exclaimed. "Anyway, I asked her what she thought she could do or what she needed from me to help. She was quiet for a bit, but then she asked if she could work on a new sales presentation. She had some ideas but didn't want to go off our script without my approval."

"Tell me more," prompted Maria again.

"That's just what I said to her! As she talked through her ideas, and I kept saying, 'tell me more,' she finally caught on. She asked me why I kept asking that question."

"Hopefully she wasn't quite as upset by that as Mike was at our meeting," Maria said, chuckling.

Elaine laughed lightly too. "No, not at all. She liked the concept and decided it was a great tool to use in her sales presentation."

"Excellent!" said Maria. She hadn't thought about that, but it made sense.

"I gave Shelly the go-ahead to try some new things this week as long as she allowed me to watch and observe. She had great success! One customer, who came in because of the ad, said he was looking around. She said, 'tell me more. What makes you just want to look around today?' Her approach was engaging and encouraging but went right to the heart of the issue. In the end, he bought new glasses *and* custom sunglasses, with all the package extras. It was amazing!"

"Elaine, that is great! I want to hear more about her approach."

"I knew you would. I'd like to schedule a call for the three of us early next week so that Shelly can talk to you directly about it. I think it would make her feel special to be able to present to you. Can you make some time?"

"Absolutely," Maria said.

When she got off the phone, Maria sat there for a minute thinking about how one little statement, 'tell me more,' could change so much. Seeing the changes in Elaine alone made her very proud.

Two weeks after the meeting, Maria heard the familiar beeps as the leadership team came online for the appointed conference call. Once everyone was on the line, she got things rolling.

"Good morning, everyone. Thank you for joining. Two weeks ago, we forged new ground in our company. We discussed getting our heads in growth mode and tackled the very real issues of communication and collaboration. I'd like to know what each of you has done to continue our mission these last two weeks. What have you learned, and what are you doing differently from what you did two weeks ago?"

Instead of silence, people were jumping in right away, fighting to be the first. It made Maria smile and feel proud.

"I can't tell you how pleased I am to hear everyone jumping in. I heard Mike first. You have the floor, Mike."

"Thanks, Maria. Good morning, everyone. I gained a lot from our meeting, despite what you might think. I want to first thank Jeff for what he shared during the meeting about how he steps-in to support his recruiters. It opened my eyes, not only in how to work with him and his team better but also in how I work with my team."

Maria started to speak, but Mike cut her off. "And, Maria, before you ask, I'd like to tell you more!"

Everyone laughed at that, and Maria, laughing herself, said, "You got it, Mike. Keep going."

Chuckling, Mike continued. "After the meeting, I thought about how busy I felt lately and started wondering if my team was missing out on anything from me if I am so busy all the time. I guess what I began wondering was, am I so busy that I don't give them enough of my time and energy? I mean, if Jeff gives up one whole day every week to support his team, what am I doing?"

"And what did you come up with, Mike?" Maria asked.

"I decided to get into my stores that are struggling right now, and instead of coming through like a tornado trying to fix things, maybe I could *do* something to fix things. I spent an entire day working in the trenches with them. And boy, did it open my eyes!"

"Tell me more!" came a voice from the line, sounding suspiciously like Jeff.

"Well, I picked our largest store in Boston. This store is in an active mall with a lot of foot traffic. We generally have a high revenue budget for this store because of its historical sales trends. As most of you know, we have been under budget for the last few months. I just got this store fully staffed, but it always seems in danger of losing people, and I didn't know why."

Maria made a murmur of understanding, and Mike continued.

"I asked the receptionist if I could sit at her desk with her, and that I would be her backup, both on the phones and with walk-ins. She was a bit nervous at first, which I understand, but within 10 minutes, I could see a problem."

Mike was on a roll, and Maria didn't even have to prompt him to continue.

"As you all know, we began to pilot internet phone lines in several of our stores, hoping for cost savings. After three calls were dropped in the first 10 minutes, and after watching the receptionist struggle to schedule appointments, I knew we had a serious problem."

Maria had already been brought into the loop on the issue and hoped Mike gave himself the credit he should as he told his story.

"I think we may be having that issue in the Aurora store too," said Jesse. "That would explain a lot."

"I bet you are," said Mike. "Or at least that you were. My folks had been complaining of the slow internet and phone line challenges for a few months, but I guess I wasn't listening. It sounded like excuses for low numbers, and I didn't give their complaints the credibility they deserved."

"I called Ron in operations right away, and he was fantastic. Thank you, Ron!"

"No problem," came Ron's deep bass voice on the line. "I am glad you brought the issue to our attention."

"What Ron isn't saying," said Mike, continuing, "is that before our meeting a few weeks ago, I probably would have called him to chew him out. But I thought about what we are trying to accomplish. I tried to be a bit more diplomatic." Mike said, laughing.

"Come on, Mike," said Ron. "You aren't giving yourself enough credit. You called to brainstorm the issue, and together we figured out something important."

"Take it away, Ron," said Mike.

"Well, I had heard some grumblings too," said Ron. "And much like Mike, I hadn't given it the attention I should have. I've been trying to control our costs in the stores with phones and internet, working with IT. Since only a couple of stores had been complaining about the phones and the internet, I assumed the issue was in the stores." Ron hadn't shared a lot during the meeting two weeks prior, but when he spoke, it held weight.

"Anyway, when Mike called, we put a few clues together. In our pilot stores, we picked three different internet carriers depending on the part of the country. We wanted to compare them in service and price. Upon investigation with Mike, the stores having trouble were with only one of the carriers. I am ashamed to say that we hadn't noticed, which tells you that we weren't watching our pilot stores at all."

Maria felt for Ron. It was hard to admit a mistake. "Ron, I hear you," she said. "We are all going to find some things as we move forward that are tough to face. But the important part is that we are learning, right?"

"Yes, you're right. We are on this now."

"But there is more," said Mike. At Maria's urging, he continued.

"My story is not about problems with Ron's team though. My story is what I learned about my team. If the Boston store is so important to me, why did I keep ignoring my team when they told me something was seriously wrong? I had to recognize that this was *my* fault. I let them down, and consequently, my receptionist fessed up later in the day that she was already submitting job applications to other businesses in the mall because she felt like she would never make her bonus if she couldn't even schedule an appointment."

"Ouch," David chimed in. "That had to hurt."

"It did, David," said Mike. "But it hurt a lot less than having to replace her. I thanked her for her honesty and asked her how I could help get things back on track, knowing that the phone and internet issue was only one of the problems. I was the other."

"Wow!" Maria said. "Mike, that is some pretty powerful stuff there. Tell us more!"

"In the end, I promised not to leave their store until the phones and internet were fixed and until they had a completely booked schedule for a week out. I spent four days in the store with them. We implemented a stand-up meeting like Jeff does with his recruiting team, and we filled the schedule. It was awesome!" Maria could hear his excitement, and others were enjoying this as well from their usually gruff colleague.

"Mike, that is fantastic," said Maria. "What is the most important thing you've learned in this exercise?"

"I now see that I spend a lot of time being busy. Don't get me wrong. I am working and working hard, but I haven't been working smart, as they say. I can still have my agenda, but if I don't listen to what my team needs in the process, I won't have a team to lead."

"And," Mike continued, "I plan to hold a stand-up meeting in each of my stores every day. I've been brainstorming with Jeff on what he does, and he has allowed me to listen in to his meetings all this week. I even had the Boston store team listen in, which they loved. It is getting us talking about how to do this better."

"Perfect. Thank you so much for that, Mike. I want to know more from you as you begin to perfect the stand-up meeting. It sounds like it is something we should consider across the board." Several voices leaned their agreement to that idea.

"OK, who else has something to share?"

A few more people chimed in with lessons learned and examples of how they were working more collaboratively with the entire leadership team. There was good energy, especially from the support services managers, who not only gave examples but also handed out lots of compliments to various sales managers.

Maria was especially proud of Kelly's input. Kelly had gone from being concerned about her job in a restructure to being excited about how they were making the company stronger.

"Well," Kelly began, "I used our 'tell me more' strategy with an irate customer."

Everyone was eager to hear this story.

"I had a customer who came in on a buy-one, get-one-half-off deal. She upgraded her frames and then added the platinum package to each pair. We all know what that means to the final purchase price and how sometimes people get sticker shock."

Grumbles from around the line proved her point was valid.

"She gave an unfavorable review on our website and asked to be contacted."

"Sounds like a challenge," said Maria. "Keep going."

"Well, when we spoke, she said we talked her into things she didn't want to buy and that the pricing wasn't up-front, and she wanted to return the glasses and get a full refund."

Unfortunately, this happened in their stores every day, which told Maria that somewhere they were missing something in the sales process. That topic was something to look at soon.

"I told her I would be happy to process her full refund if she would come and meet with me and help me to use the experience to better train my staff." Kelly laughed.

"It was a gamble, I know, but I wanted to use a little psychology with her, and I also wanted to see what I could learn if I was given

a chance to 'unpack' the issue from the customer's point of view."
Maria was tickled that the 'unpacking' concept had struck a chord
with the team.

"This is getting good," said Jesse in his slow drawl. Kelly laughed
and continued.

"I was surprised that she came in. Once they know they are going
to get a refund, people like to drop off their glasses and run out the
door." Everyone chuckled at that because it was true.

"To my surprise, she came to meet me. We sat down, and I asked her
to tell me about her experience. As she began to tell me her story
from the beginning, I continued to ask her to tell me more and kept
her talking. I did almost no talking for the first 15 minutes. And you
can all imagine how hard that was for me!" The laughter from around
the line made Maria so impressed by how this team was melding.

"After she got through every complaint, it really came down
to this: She felt that Shauna, my lead salesperson in the clinic,
didn't accurately tell her the prices as they put the order together.

"Then I began to ask some specific questions, based on what I had
learned from what she said, and I used her specific words as we
spoke. I asked her if she liked the look, feel, and comfort of her
glasses, and she said yes. I asked her if they were appropriate for
her prescription, and she said yes. I asked her if she ever purchased
glasses at prices like what she paid with us, and she said that often
she pays more."

Kelly paused for a moment to let this sink in, and Maria was struck by
the way she went through these questions with a customer.

"Then I took a real leap-of-faith. I said, 'So the primary reason you want to return your glasses, and the primary reason you feel we let you down, is because Shauna didn't provide enough specific information about price during the sales process. Correct?' The customer paused, then gave me a sheepish look, and said yes. She said, 'When you put it like that, it sounds pretty silly, doesn't it?' But I told her it wasn't silly at all, and that I didn't put it that way. I was trying to make sure I understood all her concerns. And I assured her that her refund check was printed and waiting for her with the receptionist."

"Let me guess," David said. "She kept the glasses?"

"You got it!" Kelly said happily. She apologized to me, which I told her was unnecessary, and stopped to visit with Shauna on her way out. Shauna also called me right before this conference call to tell me the woman just walked into the store now with her mother to get her mother new reading glasses."

"What a fantastic story, Kelly!" Maria said, and voices agreed and complimented her around the line. "You have shown us yet another way to use active listening to help us achieve greatness."

As everyone hopped off the line that day, Maria could feel an energy that didn't exist in the company a few weeks ago. She knew she needed to keep it going. It would be easy to fall back into old habits, but she felt confident in their progress.

Chapter 11

WALKING THE WALK

Two months later, Maria was ready to unleash the new structure to the field. Six sales directors would head up segments of the country with five or six sales managers reporting to each of them. The sales directors would report directly to Maria.

Only 10 of the current managers had officially applied for the sales director positions. Everyone else seemed to be happy with their current role, although Maria made a point to have one-on-one discussions with every manager. She didn't want anyone sitting out if they wanted to throw their hat into the ring.

Of the ten who applied, three gave her pause. David was the first. She wasn't convinced that he was ready for the job. He had too much bluster and was difficult to keep serious. Elaine was a surprise given her lack of confidence before the December meeting. Maria wasn't sure she was ready for the position yet but couldn't put the finger on why. And Dennis rounded out her list of concerns. She was most shocked that Dennis wanted the position given that it would mean more travel away from his family. He often struggled with the travel around the 10 stores in his region, and none were farther than a 2-hour drive.

After interviewing all the internal candidates, including one person from HR that had a passion for sales and had relatively appropriate management experience, Maria was confident in five of her choices. The last position, however, was still up for grabs in her mind. Elaine and David were both included in the pool of choices.

Maria was able to let Dennis down easily enough but asked him to take on some leadership assignments during the next year, so she could evaluate his potential as well as develop his areas of concern. He seemed pleased with this and felt it would give him a chance to prove himself.

The candidate from HR was not easy to let down, but she did understand the need to have people with recent and appropriate sales management experience. In the end, Maria decided to let her cover an open sales manager position in Ohio for the manager out for maternity leave in Q3. It gave everyone the chance to see what she could do.

Maria was wrapping up listening to a conference call with Jesse's region, thinking about how perfect he was for the sales director position in his part of the country. He had just finished a call with the sales specialists on add-on upgrades, piloting a new sales strategy that Maria had developed. Being able to listen like this to a manager in action gave her insight into their strengths. Jesse was an excellent leader and a great teacher, and she enjoyed watching him develop his team.

Every sales manager had begun leading these phone-training sessions. Some were very talented, and others were struggling with them, either awkward on the phone or using the calls as a monologue. Maria was doing a lot of coaching these days.

David was one who struggled with the calls, and just as if she had summoned him, she saw him calling. She jumped off Jesse's line to answer. Since David rarely called, she figured it was important to answer. What she didn't expect was to find David agitated and upset.

"Maria! I just totally screwed up. I just had my conference call. It was horrible! I messed up! What a train wreck!"

"OK, David, slow down. Tell me more." David was distraught and didn't even stop to give her grief about the line.

"I had my sales training call. I knew what I wanted to teach everyone today. No one was talking, so I kept on talking calling on people, but they barely answered, and ... "

"David, slow down. I know you're frazzled. Let's talk specifics. What was the topic?"

"I had talked with Jesse, and he shared his agenda for his call today, so I wanted to do the same thing. I told everyone that we were going to sell more add-ons and that today I was going to tell them how to do it. And no one spoke!"

"David, tell me more. Did you talk with Jesse about *how* he was going to run his call, or did you use his agenda?"

"I asked for his agenda. I know how to run these calls. I wanted to know what he was going to present."

"David, I need you to slow down. Listen to the questions I am asking you and think about *why* I am asking you. Okay?"

David was quiet for a second, obviously trying to get back under control. "I'm ready."

"David, why would I ask you if you talked to Jesse about *how* he was going to run his call?"

"Because you want me to be like him. But I know what I'm doing!"

"David, do I really want you to be just like him? Is there another reason I could ask that question?"

"OK, maybe you want to me learn from him. But I've been doing this for longer than Jesse has. I know what I'm doing!"

"David, here is a hard question for you. Let it sink in before you respond. Is it possible that in working with me on a specific pilot program to increase add-on upgrades, that Jesse might have information that you don't, both on content and on strategy?"

To his credit, David was quiet.

"All right. I can respect that. But the real problem is that no one spoke!"

"David, tell me more. Why do *you* think no one spoke?"

"I knew you were going to ask that," mumbled David. "I don't know. Maybe I was talking too much."

"OK, that is one possible reason. I wasn't on the call, so I can't know for certain. But what other possible reasons could account for people not talking?"

After a slight pause, David replied, "Maybe I wasn't clear in my message?"

"That sounds like a possibility as well, David. Anything else?"

"I don't know!" he almost wailed. "I am not sure!"

Maria realized that his level of frustration put him at the end of his ability to unpack his issue. She decided to continue the "tell me more" process to see how it went.

"David, what do you think you should do?"

Maria had never seen David like this. His natural bravado was missing, and his confidence severely shaken.

"Maria, I don't know. I am so frustrated and mad at myself, and I'm not sure what to do."

"OK. I have an idea if you would like to hear it."

"Yes!"

"You might not like my solution though. Are you still willing to hear it?" Maria had to keep from chuckling at what she intended to do. He was distraught, but she still had to get him to want her input, or else it would do no good.

"Yes, I can take it," he said a little sullenly.

"Your two main concerns are that you didn't get your message across and that no one spoke, correct?"

"Yes."

"Then if you are ready for a little humility, this is what I suggest. First, call everyone that was on the call, starting not with the person you have the best relationship with, but the person you have the weakest relationship with."

"Okay ... ," David said hesitantly.

"Say something like this. 'Look, today's call was horrible. I want to apologize. I wanted to follow-up and ask you three questions. I'd like you to be completely honest. I can take it. I *need* to take it to continue to become a better leader. First, do you know what message I wanted to get across today? Second, did I make the call something that was helpful to you in any way? And third, what advice would you give me to make these calls more dynamic so that everyone will want to interact?'"

"Oh boy," said David. "That isn't going to be easy."

"No, it won't. And the people who like you are going to want to sugar-coat things. You'll have to be strong enough to make them give you true answers. Can you do that?"

"Yes, I think I can. I get it. Be humble, ask for forgiveness, and ask them to help me to be a better leader."

"Exactly! And here is the *really* hard part. When they say something that is tough to hear, you *cannot* respond or defend. Simply practice 'tell me more.'"

"I hear you. This won't be fun, will it?"

"You might be surprised, David. Let me know how it goes!" As they hung up the phone, Maria wasn't certain if he would go through with it, or if he would try to talk to all of the people who were on the call.

When she saw her phone ring again a few hours later, it was David. She was eager to hear what he had to say.

"Well, Maria, that was painful." David laughed. "But probably one of the best things I've done in a long time."

"Tell me more, David," Maria prompted, and this time got a groan in reply.

"You were right about people being afraid to tell me the truth, so I kept on them until I got to the truth. It was tough at first, but when you hear the same theme from so many people, it is pretty hard to argue, isn't it?"

"Tell me. What was the theme?"

"Well, like you were trying to get me to realize earlier, I was talking *at* them instead of *with* them, never giving anyone a chance to chime in or discuss. So, when I *wanted* people to talk, I just wanted them to agree with me and then do what I had just been preaching. Apparently," David said with a laugh, "people want to have some input!"

Maria laughed with David, which seemed to ease his discomfort during the discussion.

"Did you get good feedback on how to improve?"

"Yes. Mack Martin even asked if he could try the new approach this week and then help me lead the call next week. He was hoping it might boost his revenue numbers for the month."

"David, that is excellent! How do you feel about having one of your team help you lead the call?"

"I think it would be great because not only is it another voice, but if someone has proven the theory, others may respect that more than just a mandate from their manager."

"I'm proud of you, David. Both for calling me today about this and for following through."

"Ah, shucks, Maria. I'm just trying to suck up to you for the sales director job!"

After they got off the phone, Maria sat for a while. She needed to announce the promotions soon and felt even more uncertain. While she was contemplating, an email popped up from Jane sharing a leadership quote. They had kept in touch, and Maria was pleased to feel she had made a new friend.

Instead of responding to the email, Maria picked up the phone and called Jane.

"Well! What a nice surprise!" came Jane's pleasant voice. "How are you?"

"I'm doing great, Jane. I think it was serendipity that your email came through. I am struggling with a decision and need some advice. Do you have a few minutes?"

"It would be a pleasure. I am just sitting here avoiding editing my new book. What's up?"

"First, as I've told you before, things have been going great. My team has grown the last couple of months. I have made decisions on five of the six promotions for the reorganization, but I can't make my mind up about the last spot."

"OK, tell me more," Jane prompted. Although she would have laughed a little at that before, Maria realized she needed to have Jane ask her that exactly.

"I have two internal candidates. One has a great deal of experience in the industry, and one has only a little more than a year in the industry."

"Does industry experience matter for the position?"

"Good question. I believe it helps, but it isn't critical."

"Tell me more about each candidate."

"David has spent his entire career in our industry, and he has been a manager for the last 10 years. He has a lot of good traits, but he tends to be more of a showman, and I'm not sure how serious he really is. I am concerned about his ability to be coached by me, and how well he'll be able to coach others."

"The other candidate?"

"Elaine is new to our industry but has more than 10 years of management experience and has managed more people and more volume than she currently has right now. In this way, she is better suited for the role. My concerns around the time I met you were about her confidence. Although she's made some great strides in the last few months, when I first met you, she was very nervous and uncertain in her role. I know her people had to see that in her too."

"You said she had made some great strides in the last few months. Give me specifics."

"I spent a full week with her in the field early December, and I saw her blossom at our planning meeting later that month. I've seen her lead a sales training in her region, and she has gained more confidence. She is much more vocal on our leadership calls, and her colleagues seem to be responding well to her suggestions and input."

"What is the most important quality you need in the job you are trying to fill?" asked Jane.

"I suppose the best way to describe it is that I need a real leader. I need someone who can lead sales managers and help them be able to lead, develop, and empower their teams. I need someone that people want to follow."

"Maria, by what you've told me so far, you already know the answer. But for some reason, you are hesitant to make the decision. Tell me more."

Maria nodded to herself. Jane was right. *I do know the answer,* she thought.

"You're right. Elaine is the right person for the position. She has proven that to me in the past few months. I guess the reason I keep considering this is because I am afraid that David will be upset and feel like he's not valued. If I had a solid external candidate, that would have made things easier."

"Would it really?" Jane asked.

"Jane, I knew there was a reason I called you. You're right again. No, it would have just allowed me an excuse not to have a very open and honest discussion with David. I believe he has potential, but I need to help him get there."

"You are headed in the right direction. Remember, I said this is simple, just not easy. Think through what you want and need to get him to understand. You'll get him there."

After they hung up, Maria jotted her thoughts down on what to say to David. It was funny how much the call helped her reach a sense of peace with her decision. And before she made any announcements, she needed to talk with David.

Chapter 12

MOVING FORWARD

The next morning, moments before her call with David, Maria took some time to review her notes and do some role-playing in her mind. She wanted to have her bullet points to review in case the call took a wrong turn.

David answered in a chipper voice. He was expecting the position, no doubt.

"Good morning, Maria! Are we ready to talk about my promotion?"

Maria anticipated this and was glad she had practiced how to start this off.

"David, I want to ask you a question. I asked you this when you came to interview formally, but now that you've had some time to think more about it, I'd like your thoughts again. Why do you want this position?"

David wasn't expecting the question, and it threw him off a bit. "Well, Maria, as I told you, I've been doing this job for years. I am qualified, and it's the position for me."

"David, those are bullet points, but they don't tell me *why* you want this position. Take out your tenure or experience. *Why* do you want *this position*?"

"Because I deserve it! I have put in my time, and I deserve this! You're not giving me the job, are you?" His voice, which had been chipper and upbeat in the beginning, was turning quickly into a pout.

"David, you still haven't answered my question, and it's critical. Let me ask you in another way. What about the position makes you want it?"

"Because I have put in my time, Maria. What would my people think if I didn't get the job?"

"Tell me more about that, David. What do you mean?"

"Well, they all know I've been here longer than almost every manager in the company. They would lose respect for me if I didn't get it." David was clearly agitated now, which Maria expected. She was a little surprised by his last answer, however.

"David, why do you think they would lose respect for you?"

"Here we go with the 'tell me more' stuff again. OK, I think my people would figure I wasn't good enough for a promotion, especially if you promote someone who has only been here a year and has never sold a pair of glasses! And if I'm not good enough for that, why should they listen to me?"

Maria was quiet for a moment, not only to keep herself calm but to slow down the conversation a bit and allow David to breathe.

"David, would it be fair to say that you want this position because it is a promotion *more* than you want the position itself?"

David wasn't quite sure what to say about that at first.

"Well, if that is the only way I'm going to get a promotion, then yes!"

Now they were onto something.

"David, if you could have or create any job in the company, what would it be? What would you enjoy doing every day? What are you passionate about?"

He answered quickly and definitively. "I would be a trainer."

That was not the answer Maria expected, but it was a start in the right direction.

"Tell me more, David. What would the job look like?"

There were a few seconds of silence before David answered. Maria was content to let it be silent. "Well, you know how in December we were brainstorming ways to get all new hires in any position up and running quickly, getting people to feel a sense of real commitment to the company?"

"Yes. I know we haven't been able to make much progress there yet, but I do want to see that happen."

"I would love to head that up. I could see myself working with the support services managers, leading orientations, heck, even helping to develop better interviewing strategies!" David had an entirely new sound to his voice.

Maria was smiling. She couldn't believe that David went from irate to energized in such a short period. He was on a roll and spoke for almost 5 minutes straight on what he'd thought about training and how it would make the company stronger. She couldn't get a word in, so she just sat back and listened until he wound himself down.

"Uh, Maria? Are you still there?"

Maria laughed. "Oh yes, David, I am. Do you see now why I started with the question that I did? Why I wanted to know *why* you wanted the sales director position?"

It was David's turn to laugh now. "Okay, I'll give you that. But I am serious. I am concerned about what people will think, and I don't want to lose a chance for a promotion."

"I'll make you a deal then. I will give you six months to see what you can do as a trainer. During that time, you'll have to juggle your current job while we see if this position is viable and makes a difference to our top line. If it is, you'll also have to help interview and train your replacement. You'll have to report to me on a regular basis, and you *must* be open to my coaching. You'll have to fully support Elaine and help her gain strength in areas that she is not as experienced. These are all my conditions. What do you say?"

"Really? What is the title? What is the pay? Can I announce my promotion today?"

Maria laughed again; now for his boyish charm and for the positive energy he exuded.

"Let me work out some details, and I will get back to you before the end of the day. I want to announce the sales director positions tomorrow, and we can announce this pilot program at the same time. Deal?"

"Deal! Maria, thank you. I know I can make this work, and I will do a great job!"

Chapter 13

COMING FULL CIRCLE

On a cold November morning, Maria walked in the door at the convention center along with thousands of other women, and a handful of men. She was only a participant this year at the 13th Annual Women's Leadership Conference; the growth in EyeSeeYou kept her hopping all over the country with no time left for volunteering. She couldn't believe how far they'd come in a year.

David was excelling in his role as Director of Corporate Training. He had implemented so many new and beneficial programs in the last seven months that she didn't know how they ever operated without them or him in the role. His leadership skills blew her away now that he was happy and, in a position that he loved.

They had some excellent nose-to-nose discussions at times, but he accepted her feedback and input, and she saw that David took his role seriously. He was extremely proud of the people he trained, and there wasn't anyone in the company who didn't know and love him. The sales directors fought over him, each wanting him in their stores as much as possible.

Elaine blossomed, and any lack of confidence she had was completely gone. She trusted in her previous work experience, bringing new and inventive strategies to the table for everyone. Maria knew that her colleagues called Elaine often, to bounce ideas off or find out how she did things in the world of medical spas.

Mark retired at the end of June and was now living full-time in Arizona. Maria knew him well enough to have seen that retirement, although his choice, was still difficult for him at times. He was openly supportive of her, and no one could have questioned his belief in her, but EyeSeeYou was his baby. It was never easy to walk away.

Maria and her husband were headed to Arizona next week to visit him, and she was looking forward to the trip. She missed his presence in the office and company and imagined that the visit would be good for them both.

Maria had just bent down to pick up a brochure that had fallen from her bag when she saw a crazy pair of neon green shoes with purple sequins walk up. With a giant, smile Maria stood up, smiling at Jane.

"I was hoping I'd find you before the day got started," she said, smiling and giving Jane a big hug.

"Me too!" said Jane. "I've got about 10 minutes before I have to check in with the speaker's lounge. You look great. How is everything?"

"Jane, I can't believe how great this year has been, and I can't believe that it's been a year since I met you. The company is doing fantastic. We are blowing our revenue budget completely out of the water, and my reorganization has been seamless. My people are achieving heights they never knew possible, all because of something that woke me up last year at this time. I cannot tell you how thankful I am that I met you!"

Jane smiled at the praise but, in her usual manner, deferred the compliment. "Maria, I just gave you a tool. You chose to use it. I have something for you," Jane said as she pulled something from her bag.

It was a hard copy of a book, *Sales Mixology: Why the Most Potent Sales and Customer Experiences Follow a Recipe for Success*, by Jane Smith.

"You finished it!"

"Yep. I didn't have it done in time for submission for this year's conference, but I'm certainly going to plug it," she said with a smile. "I wanted you to have the first official copy. I think you will enjoy it."

Maria laughed as she took the book.

"Really, Jane? You think I'll like it? Tell me more!"

ACKNOWLEDGMENTS

The process of writing this book, both in its original publication and now the second edition requires not only hard work, but it also requires you to have someone who will kick you in the pants to get things done. My husband Jeff has been that rock, that cheerleader, that proofreader, and that trainer who won't let me leave the gym (my office) without giving it my all. He doesn't allow me to settle for less than my best, no matter how many excuses I might try to give him.

I found my creative partners in Silver Tree Publishing, helping me bring this book, and books soon to follow, to life. The relationship between author and publisher is more than business. It is family. I look forward to a long and fruitful relationship with them.

Finally, I want to thank the many professionals who have impacted my career and strengthened my knowledge of what leadership truly means. I am blessed with colleagues all around the world who, every day, are beacons of excellence.

ABOUT THE
AUTHOR

Michael Sherlock is a speaker, executive leader, sales trainer and author known for her expertise in leadership, sales and the customer experience. Throughout her career, she has been successful in dealing with serious business issues by crafting them in a way that is fun, relatable, and memorable. Michael describes what she does as *Serious Business Training with Flair*.

Michael has more than 25 years of experience delivering motivational speeches and training sessions to audiences worldwide. She has a unique range of experience, from her beginnings as a Catholic school teacher to managing hundreds of people and hundreds of millions of dollars.

As a Vice President of US Sales for two global medical device companies, Michael managed net revenue exceeding $50 million annually and managed as many as 500 employees. She has built teams, hired, trained and developed both leaders and front-line sales professionals, and navigated two large companies through vast structural and operational change.

Michael Sherlock has created and executed business transformation initiatives across hundreds of businesses, built leadership development programs for numerous C-Level executives, and helped companies generate significant additional annual revenue. She set the platform for businesses to thrive both culturally and financially, through advanced leadership and vision.

In 2016, Michael published *Tell Me More*, in its 1st edition, to share her leadership mantra. The Listen, Learn and Lead concept sounds simple, and it is. But is not easy. It is not easy to change the way you think, act and react, unless or until you are willing to change your vision. Whether Michael is speaking to thousands in an annual conference, or working with a small team, she can help them do this. Today.

Today Michael leads Shock Your Potential, her Philadelphia-based training organization. She and her team provide corporations and business leaders with engaging presentations and actionable strategies on leadership, employee development, customer experience, and sales transformation. Michael shares her expertise through examples of both great successes as well as epic failures.

Michael holds a BA in Education from Eastern Washington University, and has delivered key presentations at annual conferences both within the US and internationally. Outside of her professional life, Michael is an avid urban gardener, a passionate home chef and a struggling student of the art of meditation. She enjoys traveling to countries around the world, and constantly looks forward to immersing herself in new experiences, languages, and cultures. *Tell Me More*, now in its 2nd edition, is the first book in the Shock Your Potential Series.

·

KEEP IN TOUCH!

🌐 **Learn more about Tell Me More, and quickly connect to Michael Sherlock on her website:**

ShockYourPotential.com

🎙 **Listen to the podcast:**

ShockYourPotentialPodcast.com

✉ **Send an email:**

Info@ShockYourPotential.com

@ **Find, follow, and share on social media:**

- **f** Facebook.com/MichaelSherlockSpeaks/
- 🐦 Twitter.com/MichaelSSpeaks
- 📷 Instagram.com/MichaelSherlockSpeaks
- **in** LinkedIn.com/MichaelASherlock

DON'T GO JUST YET!

Get Started Reading Book 2 of the "Shock Your Potential" Book Series!

Sales Mixology: Why the Most Potent Sales & Customer Experiences Follow a Recipe for Success

Sales Mixology continues the learning adventures started in Tell Me More. Visit www.ShockYourPotential.com to find out how to buy your copies of Michael Sherlock's other books!

SALES MIXOLOGY

By Michael Sherlock

Chapter 1
I'll Have What She's Having

Jane Smith checked into the Market Hotel in Belfast, Northern Ireland, around 10:00 a.m. on a chilly Tuesday in November. Quite to her surprise, the sun was shining brightly but she could see dark clouds all about the sky. She wasn't expecting much in terms of glorious weather.

Traveling overseas was always tiring. A relatively short, but overnight, flight (coupled with a 5-hour time change) resulted in a distinct lack of sound sleep. Nonetheless, Jane was excited to be there.

She had been invited to speak at a sales conference, taking her Tell Me More leadership principles to more than 4,000 professionals in the spa industry. Owners, managers and treatment providers would be in attendance. She was set to be on stage on Saturday as the keynote presenter. Because she had never been to Northern Ireland, and because she knew how jetlag could affect her, she had decided to go a few days early.

The hotel already had a room waiting for her, and she gladly embraced a rare morning nap.

That afternoon, she explored the city by foot, wandering the cobblestone streets. She enjoyed a bowl of chowder and a pint of Beamish at a small place with a large and roaring fire. She was in heaven.

While she ate, she plotted out her next couple of days, knowing that a Black Taxi tour and the Titanic museum were on her must-do list. But she knew that she also didn't want to overdo it on her first day while battling time changes. That could be a recipe for disaster.

Deciding to make it a simple and casual evening, she took the concierge's suggestion that she enjoy Fred's Jazz & Cocktail Lounge in the hotel. The day had turned to a bitterly cold rain, and staying in seemed like a good idea. Jane could have a light meal, enjoy some music and then release her exhaustion to the giant soaking tub and enormous comfy bed. The concierge also told her that Fred's had one of the most impressive cocktail menus around, which piqued her interest.

Walking into Fred's was like walking back in time. Deep red velvet-covered chairs and red leather couches dotted the landscape. The dark wood walls gave a sense of warmth and beauty that made Jane wonder if she was dressed appropriately.

One of the joys of traveling to Ireland, so far, had been people's complete acceptance of her wildly colored hair. Surprising hair colors were one of her trademarks. Currently white blond with deep purple roots, she felt almost royal inside the walls of this velvety cocktail lounge. Except for her jeans, of course.

She sat at the bar. She always sat at the bar when she traveled.

Travel could be a lonely thing. Sitting at a bar allowed her to be around people, gaining a sense of community. She could engage, or not, depending on what she felt like. Jane also felt it unfair to be solo at a table, knowing a server could have two or more people, and thus an opportunity for the server to earn a bigger tip.

The place was humming, alive with people and laughter and buzzing conversations. And from the bar, she could watch it all.

Despite the busyness of the bar, and what she was noticing as both a cocktail station and floor show, a bartender came to her almost immediately. His warm smile was the first welcome.

"Welcome to Fred's. My name is Ken. I will take care of you tonight, along with my colleagues. May I ask your name?"

Jane was impressed just by that. Sure, she had experienced similar welcomes before. In fact, every time she went through the Atlanta airport, she tried to stop by the P.F. Chang's in Terminal A. They always asked your name, gave you theirs and then placed a little tent card to remind you of their names. Out of curiosity once, she picked up the card and flipped it over. "Jane" was written on the back along with the words "club soda with lime." Brilliant!

She had been working on getting better at remembering names when meeting someone new. Sometimes her brain was a few steps ahead of her, allowing the name to slip just past her awareness. It wasn't a trait she was proud of, and she was determined to get better at it.

"Hello Ken. My name is Jane."

"Welcome Jane. I can see this is your first time. Would you allow me to give you a tour of our menu?"

"Absolutely! You obviously make beautiful cocktails. I have no idea what to order."

"Jane, you are not alone. We have several wonderful and delicious things. Let's find out what suits you best tonight."

Wow, thought Jane. *I am even more impressed!*

Jane didn't mean to make this dinner a learning opportunity, but it had already given her several key thoughts. First, she realized that, unlike the bartenders at P.F. Chang's, Ken did not write her name down, but he had repeated her name twice. That seemed significant and very similar to a strategy she was trying that prompts you to use someone's name three times in the first few minutes of an introduction.

Second, Ken's method of asking permission to give her a tour of the menu pulled at something in her brain. And based on his last statement, she was wondering if he employed a similar strategy to her *tell me more* principles.

"Tour away Ken!" Jane said with a smile.

"Before I begin, let me ask you a couple of questions. Do you normally prefer a cocktail, beer, glass of wine or something non-alcoholic?"

Jane was a little surprised by the question, if only because so often bartenders lead with house specials or their favorites to pour or mix. Sometimes they simply put a menu in front of you and walk away. That always felt so sterile.

"Great question Ken. I like all the above depending on the circumstance. But I think I would like to start out with a cocktail."

"Excellent!" Ken said with a smile as he flipped a few pages into the menu. "Now, some of the cocktails here are old favorites." He pointed to the first list. "Some are adaptations, and some are completely unique creations. But if there is anything that you would like that isn't listed, we can make that happen for you. As you can see," Ken swept his arm back to indicate an assortment of glass bottles and jars of all shapes and sizes, "we have an extensive supply of bitters, aromatics, syrups, herbs and spices. Some days I feel more like a scientist than a bartender," he said smiling.

Jane could understand that statement. The vials were large and small. — some with glass stoppers, some with eyedroppers, some with tiny spoons resting on top. Each drew her eye and interest.

It was at this point that Jane realized how many new people had arrived, and how much time she was taking with Ken. She felt guilty. He seemed to sense her unspoken question and said "Don't worry, Jane. Everyone will be well taken care of. Right now, you are my only customer."

Jane was taken aback. He really seemed to mean it. He had no sense of stress, and his focus was not drawn elsewhere. But what she did notice right then was the addition of two more bartenders, greeting the new arrivals. It was like they magically multiplied to meet the needs of the guests.

Bringing her attention back to the menu, Ken asked another probing question. "Now tell me a bit about you. Are you partial to one kind of liquor over another? Or are there any liquors you don't particularly care for?"

Jane thought for a moment before she responded, not because she didn't have an answer, but because she was trying to fix his questions and their tone in her mind.

She'd been asked that question before, but almost with a bored slant as if the bartender were trying to cut down the list to get to a solution fast and easy. Ken, however, seemed to be using his questions, and her answers, to develop a profile from which he could launch solutions. It was very much like *tell me more*, but more direct.

Ken, however, seemed to be using his questions, and her answers, to develop a profile from which he could launch solutions. It was very much like *tell me more*, but more direct.

"I am pretty daring," said Jane as she pointed to her hair. Ken nodded and smiled.

"But I suppose the only thing I am really not a fan of is Scotch. It tastes like drinking a leather couch."

That made Ken laugh heartily, and Jane smiled back.

"OK Jane, I hear you. You don't like peaty Scotch. Which makes it a great thing that you are in Northern Ireland and not Scotland!" They both laughed while another bartender came to ask Ken a question. But instead of her talking to Ken first, she looked at Jane and said "Please accept my apology. Would it be alright if I stole Ken for just one moment?" Jane was flabbergasted!

"Of course!" said Jane, feeling quite respected. Before they left, however, Ken introduced the two.

"Jane, I would like you to meet Jacqueline. She is our Director of Training. Jacqueline, this is Jane. We are narrowing down her cocktail."

"Very nice to meet you!" Jacqueline said, offering a hand to shake. "I promise to only steal Ken for a heartbeat."

Jane nodded agreement and the two stepped over to the grand central station for mixology. They put their heads together, coming to an apparent agreement, and then Ken was back.

"Jane, I apologize for the interruption. Shall we continue?"

Through a series of other questions, Jane felt that Ken had her profile established. Then he knocked her socks off yet once again.

"Jane, there are several cocktails on our menu that I think you will enjoy. Tell me what you would prefer. Would you like to browse the menu on your own to decide? Would you like to have me make some suggestions? Or would you like to trust me to make something unique just for you?"

That sealed the deal. There was only one choice. Although she did relish the fact that she was given the opportunity to *make* that choice.

"Create away Ken. My cocktail is in your hands!"

And with that, Ken smiled, left her the menu to peruse and went in search of ingredients. When he returned with bottles and vials, stemware and a fruit bowl, a lighter and chunks of raw sugar, Jane knew she was in for a treat.

Watching Ken build the cocktail, she could clearly see his passion for the little things. She was certain this would be a rendition of an Old Fashioned, one of her favorites, but some of his ingredients were quite surprising.

From time to time, he would glance up, smile and return to his masterpiece. It didn't take long, and yet she felt like she had been privy to a private show. A play just for her.

In the background, she could hear the band getting ready to start their set. It seemed simply perfect all the way around.

After the orange rind had been twisted, heated and rubbed around the rim of the glass, Ken presented her with the cocktail.

"I would suggest you let it sit for just a moment to settle the flavors and allow the ice to become one with the drink," Ken said, smiling because he saw how eager she looked to taste it.

"And of course, smell it. See if you can determine some of the flavors and the way they begin to blend."

Jane smiled, smelled, closed her eyes and was impressed with the overall effect. When she finally gave into her temptation to taste it, she savored the first notes on her tongue. Her smile was all Ken needed.

"I'm going to assume that means you like it?" Ken teased.

"Absolutely!" Jane replied. "This has been amazing so far. If the food is anything like this, I am in for a treat tonight."

"Yes, you are," replied Ken. "Would you like to see a menu right away, or would you like to enjoy this for a while?"

Jane loved the question again. It put her back in the driver's seat and gave Ken vital information without his having to make assumptions.

"Ken, I think I would like to enjoy this and the music for a bit first."

"Perfect Jane. Just catch my eye when you would like a menu."

Although she was engrossed in the music, she noted that Ken would often glance her way to see if she was ready to proceed with her meal.

He was never intrusive, and never neglected her. She wondered how he perfected that balance.

Although she was engrossed in the music, she noted that Ken would often glance her way to see if she was ready to proceed with her meal. He was never intrusive, and never neglected her. She wondered how he perfected that balance.

She had a wonderful meal and realized that she hadn't enjoyed an evening out quite as much in a long time. The whole experience got her brain buzzing with ideas and excitement. Every part of the evening provided her with other examples of excellence, and she jotted down notes on at least six cocktail napkins. It was getting kind of absurd, actually.

Just then, the band announced a short break. Ken was busy removing Jane's dinner dishes and she was contemplating that giant bathtub and a full night of deep sleep when Jacqueline popped into her field of vision.

"Hello Jane. How are you enjoying your evening?"

"Jacqueline, this has been absolutely lovely on so many levels!"

Jacqueline looked quizzically down at Jane's stack of impressive napkin notecards, making Jane laugh at the unspoken question.

"I suppose it's a hazard of the job." Jane said. "I'm a business writer and a speaker."

"Really?" Jacqueline said. "What do you write about specifically?"

"I focus on leadership, sales and the customer experience. And man, have I found the trifecta here tonight," Jane said with a smile.

"I'd like to know more about that. Do you mind if I join you for a moment?" Jacqueline asked.

"Please do!" Jane replied enthusiastically. "Would you mind if I asked you a few questions?" Jane asked as Jacqueline made her ways around the bar to take the seat next to Jane.

"Fire away."

"First of all, my experience here tonight has been exceptional. It has been an overwhelmingly positive customer experience. How do you make this happen?"

"Well Jane, before I answer that question, let me ask you another first. What is it about your experience that has made it such an over-whelmingly positive experience?"

Jane had to laugh to herself. This was getting better every minute.

"Well, I suppose first, I have been blown away by the personal atten-tion I have had from Ken, you and the entire team. This place is packed, and yet I feel like I am the only customer. How do you create that environment?"

Now it was Jacqueline's turn to laugh. "Great question Jane. And I am so pleased to hear that we delivered our core promise to you. The cocktails, food and music are all exquisite. But they mean nothing if we do not deliver an unforgettable and personal experience."

Jane nodded in agreement. "I see what you mean. There are lots of places where I have enjoyed the food or the music or the cocktails, but not all of them draw me back again for another visit."

"Exactly," Jacqueline said smiling. "That is my responsibility here with this team. I expect a lot out of them. But mostly I expect them to believe that it is vital that we deliver on that experience. I take a long time to make hiring decisions because I want to make sure we have the absolute right people."

"Wait," Jane said. "I don't want this to come out wrong, but I thought Ken said you were the trainer. Aren't hiring decisions made by the manager?"

Jacqueline smiled. "No offense taken. We do things a bit differently here, for a reason. See that woman over there by the kitchen?" Jane nodded when she saw the woman in a deep blue dress speaking with one of the chefs. "That is Sandra, the restaurant manager. She is responsible for how the entire business performs. But she holds the rest of us responsible for the parts we play."

Jacqueline had to smile at Jane's confused look.

"Let me see if I can explain better. The Executive Chef is responsible for the quality of our menu, but his Sous Chef is responsible for making sure the kitchen runs smoothly every day to achieve that. The Director of Mixology is responsible for the variety and quality of our bar selections, but Ken, our Bar Lead is responsible for making sure the bar meets all customer expectations. Both the Sous Chef and Ken screen candidates for their team, but I make the ultimate decisions on all hiring because I am responsible for making sure whoever we hire will be trained to our expectations. Does that make sense?"

It did, and Jane nodded, but she was surprised as well.

"I think I see where you are going here," said Jane. "The larger vision is held responsible at every level in the business. But at the end of the day, unless someone is willing and able to be trained, no matter their resume, you don't want them on the team. Is that right?"

Jane knew she was on to something when Jacqueline nodded as she finished her thought.

"Yes!" said Jacqueline. "It means that we all must have common vision and purpose. No one can be out just for themselves. They must see that we are trying to make something greater than just a meal or a cocktail or a night of great jazz. We all have to be committed to the single purpose of the overall experience."

Jane was smiling and jotting more notes on napkins. Out of the corner of her eye, she noticed the General Manager walking toward Jacqueline. She was afraid she had already taken up too much time again, but neither woman seemed disturbed.

Jacqueline took the opportunity to introduce the women. "Sandra, I'd like to introduce you to Jane. She is a business writer and speaker and has been enjoying how we do business here. She was just picking my brain on a few things." Jane couldn't help but feel just a bit guilty. She hoped she wasn't encroaching on trade secrets. She said as much, and both women chuckled.

"No worries at all Jane!" Sandra said with a giant smile. "We are very proud of what we do here, but there are no secrets. Just hard work, mutual respect and a completely aligned vision."

"It certainly seems that way," Jane said, and then embarrassed herself with a yawn. That got both women laughing again as well. "I am so sorry! I think the travel, time change and great food has finally caught up to me. I hope you don't mind if I come back again tomorrow to observe and maybe ask some more questions!" Jane said with a smile.

"We would be happy to have you again Jane." Jacqueline said. "I am not sure what you have on your agenda tomorrow, but if you are available in the morning, I have a new hire training from 9:00 a.m. to 5:30 p.m. tomorrow. You would be welcome to sit in and observe for as much, or as little, as you would like." Sandra was nodding her agreement as well.

"I would love that!" Jane said. "What an offer!"

"Fantastic. Meet here in the bar at 9 o'clock sharp. I think you'll have fun."

As Jane said goodnight to both women and headed toward her room, she couldn't help but be excited about the opportunity in front of her. As she crawled into bed, she glanced at the stack of cocktail napkins with notes written on every inch of open space. She laughed and made a mental note to take her notebook with her tomorrow.

Made in the USA
Columbia, SC
25 April 2022

59440807R00130